Kelly -- Andy

True Faith Keeps You Going

When Things Get Tough

Also in the Deeper Devotions Series:

It's Who You Are That Counts

DEEPER *devotions*

True Faith Keeps You Going

WHEN THINGS GET TOUGH

James

JAMES LONG

ZondervanPublishingHouse
Grand Rapids, Michigan

A Division of HarperCollins*Publishers*

When Things Get Tough

Requests for information should be addressed to:

ZondervanPublishingHouse
Grand Rapids, Michigan 49530

Library of Congress Cataloging-in-Publication Data

Long, James, 1949–
When things get tough : true faith keeps you going / James Long.
p. cm. — (Deeper devotions)
ISBN: 0-310-20598-0 (pbk.)
1. Suffering—Religious aspects—Christianity—Biblical Teaching. 2. Bible. N.T. James—Devotional literature. 3. Teenages—Prayer—books and devotions—English. I. Title. II. Series.
BS2785.4.L64 1997
248.8'6—dc21 97–24968
CIP

Interior design by Sue Vandenberg Koppenol

Printed in the United States of America

97 98 99 00 01 02 03 04 /❖ DC/ 10 9 8 7 6 5 4 3 2 1

In memory of my father,
who gave me more
than I realized

Aim at heaven
and you get earth thrown in.
Aim at earth
and you get neither.

—C. S. Lewis

Contents

How to Use This Book

- You can simply read it. Front to back.
- You can read each chapter complete in one sitting.
- Or you can skip around, checking out what interests you.

But if you want to get the most out of this book, try this:

- Read the section marked **"Weekend Reading"** at one sitting when you have a bit more time. Perhaps on a Saturday or Sunday afternoon. Each "Weekend Reading" section introduces an important theme and develops it with a true-life story and some thoughts from the Bible. Make that theme your spiritual project for the week, whether the topic is hardship, temptation, hypocrisy, prayer. Whatever. There are fourteen weekly themes in this book.
- Next, take a few minutes each day to remind yourself of the theme, using the one-page **"Daily Checkpoints."** Following each chapter, you will find these "Checkpoints" marked Monday, Tuesday, Wednesday, Thursday, Friday. You can read these pages and give some thought to the week's theme, even if you have only a few minutes to devote. This will help you develop the habit of setting aside some time each day to think about your faith. You can spend more time, of course. Each day's reading introduces

questions, points you to a Bible passage, guides you into a prayer focus. It would be excellent to follow these readings with an open notebook, jotting down insights and questions as you go along.

- It would be helpful several times during the week to take another fresh look at the "Weekend Reading" section. Keep your mind focused on the personal project for the week, the theme of each chapter. You just may find your life changing, little by little, as you remind yourself of God's loving concern and the kind of faith that will keep you going, even when things get tough.

Acknowledgments

Some words of thanks for some great friends

For many years, *Campus Life* magazine was the home for my writing—a place to express my thoughts and develop my skills. Among the things that most helped in that process were capable editors—who also became my friends—and loyal, energetic readers, whose questions and observations improved the magazine and sharpened my own thinking. A particular word of thanks is due Tim Stafford and Gregg Lewis, friends and gifted writers, who have encouraged me, and set me straight more than a few times. Some of the words that have found their way into this book first appeared in the pages of *Campus Life*, and I am grateful for the permission to reprint them here.

The manuscript was read and keyboarded by my friend Marie Gomez. Once again, the words "accurate," "efficient," "wise," and "thoughtful" come to mind. Some things never change.

Dave Lambert edited the book—which was fun for me, because it's been my privilege to work with Dave on a number of projects over the years. I have learned to value his editorial opinion as well as his friendship.

Harriet, my wife and best friend for life, has virtually *defined* love and encouragement for me. I would not want to attempt anything without her partnership. Not just because her counsel improves what I do but also because it's just plain more fun that way.

James Long

[illegible]

[illegible]

[illegible]

[illegible]

[illegible]

First Words

Advice from a Friend

If the Brother of Jesus Could Talk to You

What about hardship, temptation, hypocrisy? And can you explain God's will, money, patience, prayer?

They had questions about their faith, those first Christians. They faced hardship and temptation. They talked too much—their words got them into trouble. At times, they could have been accused of hypocrisy and discrimination. They found prayer confusing and sometimes got their priorities twisted around. They needed guidance and encouragement.

In other words, they were a lot like us.

So James wrote them a letter.

You would have liked James. It seems everyone did—those in the church and those outside. And James would have understood you. For a time, he was confused about faith. Jesus was his half-brother; they grew up in the same home. He saw all those amazing things his brother did. What he didn't see, he most certainly heard about. And yet, for years he did not believe. Kind of like those of us who spend years going to church, hanging out around Christians, figuring there may be some truth to it, but never quite taking the plunge.

When the crowds turned against Jesus and things so quickly went downhill, James saw it coming. I rather doubt he was surprised, even by the crucifixion. What did surprise him was a visit from his brother *after* the crucifixion. After the resurrection. Like many of us—perhaps like *you*—the time came when it all made sense. Faith was fact. Jesus was Lord.

Soon, James rose to leadership in that early church, along with Peter, John, and later Paul. He had a rather amazing reputation. People started calling him "James the Just" because his faith was so consistent, his love for God so deep, his life so full of goodness. People talked about his prayer too. They said he prayed so much that his knees were hard-skinned like a camel's.

In time, people turned on him, just as they had turned on Jesus, his brother, and he was martyred for his faith. The religious leaders outside the church were so angered by his faith and preaching that they threw him off the roof of the Temple, then stoned him, then beat him with a club. His final words before his death echoed the last words of his brother, spoken years before: "Father, forgive them, for they know not what they do."

Here then is advice from a friend. Answers to some of our most pressing questions, from the brother of Jesus.

Week 1

Hardship

James 1:1–12

When Things Get Tough

News of a serious accident swept through the school, raising the inevitable question: Why?

She sat near me in art class. I didn't know her well, though we became casual friends, delving into "philosophical discussions" as we worked. I do recall that her forte was calligraphy, and the letterforms she created were near-perfect. Uniform, precise. Just watching her work, I knew she loved order.

Aside from these things, I remember little else about her, except how she reacted when we were told in class that a student from our school had been killed in a head-on collision. She did not know the guy. None of us did. Even so, we were all stunned. In the talk that followed, I could tell that, for most, the shock was mixed with a sort of morbid curiosity about the crash. But her questions, true to the spirit of our philosophical discussions, focused on what kind of world would permit such tragedy. I was impressed by the sensitive way she viewed this loss: in her mind, a great, irreplaceable, artistic masterpiece—a life—had been destroyed. Why?

I watched her that afternoon as the initial shock wore off. She lifted her pen, dipped it in ink, and bent over a piece of illustration board, intent on bringing life to some idea, though she was preoccupied with questions larger than life itself. And the questions lingered; they rose spontaneously in conversation during the next few weeks. She craved, as I think we all did, some reassurance that life itself had more purpose than it sometimes seemed. In a world in which cars veer off course and collide, where was God, in all his artistic order and precision?

The difficulties we face are not always so dramatic. Whether death or sickness, family problems or friendship hassles, struggles with grades or questions about the future—a similar question hides behind each one. How do we make sense out of hardship?

If you could send questions to God like you can to some advice columnist, sooner or later most of us would get around to this one: Why?

And though God doesn't quite fill in that blank, at least he is not silent on the subject of suffering. In fact, he has so much to say about hardship that you get the impression he was not surprised by it. That he fully expected it.

Which he did.

So, what's his perspective?

Hardships come with purpose.

I don't buy the idea that God causes hardship; that seems to be against his nature. On the other hand, he certainly does make use of it, as if he won't let even the difficult things we face be wasted. They set a process in motion that improves our character.

Now, if this process means I must hurt, as it often does, I might never choose hardship. Yet afterward, seeing the good that came as a by-product of my struggles, I may find my resentment fading.

In fact, God's ability to bring good out of bad is so strong that the words "joys" and "trials" can be used in the same sentence, without seeming ridiculous.

> *"Consider it pure joy, my brothers, whenever you face trials of many kinds, because you know that the testing of your faith develops perseverance. Perseverance must finish its work so that you may be mature and complete, not lacking anything"* (James 1:2–4).

God is ready to help us through any circumstance, regardless of how difficult.

At times my hardships threaten to crush me. I am confused, uncertain how to react, what to say, what to do. God seems remote. Doubts of his love and wisdom creep in.

I find it reassuring that when difficulties confuse me, God asks me to turn toward him, not from him. Through the Bible, and in my past experiences in which he has shown his care, I hold a picture of God as trustworthy, regardless of my confusing circumstances. When I feel that first edge of doubt, he urges me to turn my back on it and to look instead at that picture of his trustworthiness. He also invites me to ask for strength and wisdom, a request he promises to grant. He may not take away the circumstance that caused my doubt, but he will give me reason to trust.

He may not bail me out of the problem, but he does promise to stay close and to help me cope.

> *"If any of you lacks wisdom, he should ask God, who gives generously to all without finding fault, and it will be given to him. But when he asks, he must believe and not doubt, because he who doubts is like a wave of the sea, blown and tossed by the wind. That man should not think he will receive anything from the Lord; he is a double-minded man, unstable in all he does" (James 1:5–8).*

We can put life and its hardships in a new perspective.

I like to think of heaven as the place where values get inverted. Things that seem important here and now get flipped around, so they can be viewed from a different, better, more accurate perspective. God does have another angle on life, hard for me to see now. Is there anything in this life that makes it easier to sort out what really matters? Is there any type of experience that shows me the difference between what is temporary and what is permanent?

Yes. Hardship does that. It forces questions that might otherwise never occur to me in this life. The questions bring me to the Bible, where I find a new, higher viewpoint. A different angle on all I experience, both the good and the bad.

Imagine this: We reside on the ground floor of Forever. We know a little of the final outcome of all that matters. And we can pick what we consider important, realizing what does and does not have real, lasting value.

> *"The brother in humble circumstances ought to take pride in his high position. But the one who is rich should take pride in his low position, because he will pass away like a wild flower. For the sun rises with scorching heat and withers the plant; its blossom falls and its beauty is destroyed. In the same way, the rich man will fade away even while he goes about his business" (James 1:9–11).*

Our patience in hardship is not forgotten by God, or ignored.

He knows what hurts us. And he knows how we handle it.

When time, which seems like forever, is swallowed up by what actually *is* forever—timelessness—I will face a wise and loving God. Maybe then I will ask, "Why?" Maybe then I will know, without asking. Maybe then I will be able to trust my questions to his love and wisdom, without insisting on answers.

In any case, until then, he patiently urges me to trust him with my hardships and with the hardships of others. In exchange, he promises his help now. And later, he says, he will not forget.

> *"Blessed is the man who perseveres under trial, because when he has stood the test, he will receive the crown of life that God has promised to those who love him" (James 1:12).*

As I think back on that strange afternoon in art class—when bad news came to us—I imagine God agreeing with my friend: a great, irreplaceable artistic masterpiece—a life—had been destroyed. In this ruined world, waiting for his artistic touch to restore it, unthinkable hardship happens.

Because we know suffering, it is reasonable to ask: "God, can you make sense out of this?"

Because we know the promise of a loving God, it is reasonable that he should ask us: "Can you trust me as you wait for answers?"

Monday Checkpoint: *Hardship*

To live life is to face hardship. It is not surprising that we would ask, "Why?"

Think about it . . .

Remember the times you have faced something difficult? It may not have been some major life-and-death issue. Maybe it was "just" the breakup of a friendship. Maybe you overheard your parents fighting and it caused you worry or fear. Maybe it was the disappointment of not making the team or not getting the job or being turned down by your first-choice college. An illness you faced. A sick grandparent.

Or maybe it *was* a life-and-death issue. A friend who faced serious disease or a devastating accident. The death of a parent, the disintegration of a family.

Whether it's something as simple as a bad grade or as dramatic as a terminal illness, we all know what it is to face disappointment, discouragement, difficulty. We all have our hardships.

When those times strike, it is not surprising that we would voice the one-word question "Why?" In fact, "Why?" can be a pretty good question if you're asking the right person. As we sort through our feelings, our questions, even our doubts, it is good to remind ourselves that a loving God shares our concerns.

God's Word says . . .

"If God is for us, who can be against us?" (Romans 8:31).

Make it a prayer . . .

Thank you, Lord, that even in my times of question or doubt, you never turn me away. You are always as close as my very breath.

Tuesday Checkpoint: *Hardship*

Who would ever put the words "joy" and "hardship" in the same sentence? God would. But why?

☞ Think about it . . .

It is astounding to think that God is big enough to bring something good out of something bad. It's not that he would create painful circumstances, then push us into them. Life is already painful in a world at odds with God. Just living on this planet puts us in the path of hardship. Yet God takes a personal interest in us and in everything we experience.

We will encounter hardship. We will experience pain. We will face disappointment. These challenging times will bring frustration, but they do not also have to be wasted. God will use them to bring good. They will make us stronger. In fact, God is so skillful at bringing something positive out of the most negative of circumstances that it can even stir a sense of joy just anticipating the good that he will do, even in the face of all that pain.

☞ God's Word says . . .

"Consider it pure joy . . . whenever you face trials of many kinds, because you know that the testing of your faith develops perseverance" (James 1:2–3).

☞ Make it a prayer . . .

Lord, the next time hardship strikes, turn my attention toward you. In the midst of my disappointment, give me a glimpse of joy.

Wednesday Checkpoint: *Hardship*

Is God big enough to handle my fears and patient enough to endure my doubts?

☞ Think about it . . .

What happens when the bad news comes? You lose the job. Or flunk the test. Or find that a friend has turned against you. What happens when the news is worse than bad? Your dad's out of work. Or your parents are fighting . . . again. Or you get the word of your grandmother's illness or a friend's serious accident.

Bad news comes, shock follows. It can be difficult just trying to sort out your feelings, your thoughts. Doubts and fears may cloud your mind and muddle your thinking. Sometimes bad news calls for a response, and it's hard to know what to think, what to say, what to do. If there was just someone to talk to—someone who cares, someone with the wisdom you can't quite find.

Isn't that precisely what God promises to do for us? To listen and to respond?

☞ God's Word says . . .

"If any of you lacks wisdom, he should ask God, who gives generously to all without finding fault, and it will be given to him" (James 1:5).

☞ Make it a prayer . . .

I do not know what I will face as the next day unfolds. Lord, give me the wisdom this day will demand.

Thursday Checkpoint: *Hardship*

We live on the ground floor of "forever." Heaven is the upper story. From that angle, life would look completely different.

☞ Think about it . . .

If you look at things on the surface, life's problems seem fairly ea$y to $olve. With enough money, for instance, life gets comfortable. Think of all the problems that go away if you can just throw some money at them. All the comfort it brings. Flash those bills and you find people even treat you better. Your money does buy a measure of popularity.

On the other hand, there is something about life that levels us. Something that puts the rich and the not-so-rich on equal footing. Hardship does that. *Time* does that, when enough time goes by. Then the discovery unfolds: The things we once thought so important, and the things we once overlooked as insignificant, may trade places. We look at things from a different angle, and now they are not all they once appeared to be.

Heaven will shift our perspective like that. Completely. It will show us what we should have considered valuable. If we want a sneak preview, all we need to do is study the Bible. In it, the great secrets of life unfold.

☞ God's Word says . . .

"The brother in humble circumstances ought to take pride in his high position" (James 1:9).

☞ Make it a prayer . . .

Lord, as I face today and the hardship it may bring, fill my mind with your thoughts, your priorities, your values.

Friday Checkpoint: *Hardship*

God sees your hardship and never forgets your faith.

Think about it . . .

Some disappointments are heavier than others. They weigh us down so much, we wonder if we will ever be able to carry them. We wonder if we will ever recover from their weight. But even minor hardships are a burden. Disappointment is hard to hold.

Imagine this: Before life dumps its pain on you, God feels the weight. Before you are burdened down, God tests the hardship. Is it too heavy? Are you too weary?

Imagine this: While you are carrying that frustration, the unseen arms of God are under it, lifting some of that weight. It would have been a crushing heartache, but somehow you are able to stand up under it.

God knows what you are facing today, and he knows how much harder it is to face today, if yesterday was also painful. He knows your disappointment, and he knows you. He understands that life is sometimes a struggle, and he will never forget your faith.

God's love for you has no limit. He merely asks that you love him in return and that you trust him in your hardship.

God's Word says . . .

"Blessed is the man who perseveres under trial, because when he has stood the test, he will receive the crown of life that God has promised to those who love him" (James 1:12).

Make it a prayer . . .

Lord, keep my faith strong regardless of my circumstances.

Week 2

Temptation

James 1:13–15

Weekend Reading

Why Do I Want to Do What's Wrong?

> If God created us with these obvious weaknesses, why do we get the blame instead of him?

Jeff describes his anger like this:

"I just feel this pressure building, like a volcano. I know I'm going to explode, but I don't know how to hold it back. Well, to be truthful, sometimes I do know how to hold it back, if I decide to soon enough. But at the time I am so frustrated that I just don't want to control myself. It is like I need the release. So I wind up screaming at someone, looking for just the right words that will hurt the most. Afterward, I feel so embarrassed and ashamed I want to hide where no one can find me."

Brad's problem is different. Unlike Jeff, he can handle his temper, but Brad's thought-life is out of control. When he's alone, he finds himself falling into a detailed world of sexual fantasy he's created through the magazines he reads and the videos he watches.

"At the time," Brad says, "there is nothing I want more than to get a 'lust fix.' That's what it's like, you know, a sort of addiction. When I'm with friends and we're watching a video, we kind of laugh it off, like it's just entertainment or something. But it's more than that to me. The real problem is when I'm completely alone. All these images from the magazines and videos come back to me, like I am showing reruns on the screen of my mind. Later on, I feel guilty—real guilty—and I wonder if it's possible to change."

Amy talks about her recurring struggle but begins by explaining she never really thought of it as "temptation" or "wrong." Only recently has she seen it as something destructive to her and to others.

"What I find myself struggling with is other people. What I mean is, I compare myself to them. If they are more attractive or more popular or whatever, I look for their flaws. It's like if I can discover their faults, I won't feel inferior to them. Then I find little ways to mention their weaknesses to my friends. And when I see someone at school, or even at church, who is kind of strange or not too good-looking, I really notice them. Sort of laugh behind their back. It makes me feel better about myself. I've thought this way about people for a long time in the back of my mind. I wasn't even aware I was doing it. Now that I'm aware of it, I feel guilty a lot. I used to feel pretty good about myself; now I feel all dirty inside."

Wrong is not God's nature.

Being God, he is perfect, I assume. Yet, I remember wondering: if God is so great, why did he make me so vulnerable to temptation? If he wants me to stand, why did he make it so easy for me to fall? If he programmed me to sin—and it sure seems that way—

why do I get the blame instead of him? If he is all-powerful and yet he built these weaknesses into me, isn't he a greater tempter than the devil?

Sometimes you can read something repeatedly without its meaning sinking in. Then one day, out of the blue, the point hits you. I don't have all the philosophical questions worked out ("What is the source of evil?" for instance), but I read this verse in the Bible that helped me put the question in a different perspective.

> *"When tempted, no one should say, 'God is tempting me.' For God cannot be tempted by evil, nor does he tempt anyone" (James 1:13).*

These two sentences tell me that temptation is a foreign idea to God. God never invites me to sin, and deep wrongdoing doesn't appeal to him like it does to me. When it comes to temptation and sin, God and I speak different languages altogether.

This makes some sense to me. It certainly does not answer all my questions, but I can accept the idea that my desire for wrong is not his fault. I now wonder if maybe my power of choice is stronger than I ever imagined.

Wrongdoing *is* my nature.

So is wrong thinking. By that I mean it comes naturally to me. It is not surprising that Jeff should struggle with anger or Brad with lust or Amy with envy. A downward pull is wired into all of us. There are different kinds of temptations that, well, *tempt* us. But when the Bible wants to describe the process of temptation, it uses a metaphor we understand quite well: sexual desire.

"Each one is tempted when, by his own evil desire, he is dragged away and enticed. Then, after desire has conceived, it gives birth to sin; and sin, when it is full-grown, gives birth to death" (James 1:14–15).

Brad may readily identify with this picture. He has felt the desire pulling him away, enticing him. Maybe he had homework to do but read something else instead. He could have rented a decent video but felt that pull to find something that showed a bit more skin. Perhaps he has even acted out his fantasies in his relationships.

The Bible does take the image further, beyond a mental struggle: the desire is acted on, the relationship consummated; a child is born. The "father" was evil desire, the "offspring" was sin. Then the child grows to adulthood and has a child of its own: sin's child is death.

Anger and envy, dishonesty and pride; whatever the temptation, it follows this same path. It begins with enticement. Flirting with a wrong thought. But once we act on it, a deathly process is set in motion. Sooner or later, that anger or envy, dishonesty or pride, hurts us deeply.

What does God do about my wrong?

If God does not tempt me, what does he do? I pulled out a tablet and began listing answers to that question. Here's what I came up with:

God gives me everything I truly need long before I ever sin. In giving me what I need, he makes sin unnecessary. James 1:16–18 talks about God's good gifts to us. Or think of the story of Adam and Eve in their garden paradise. Their needs were met by God, so that sin did not have to happen. It's the same for us.

God gave me a conscience, his laws, and his Spirit to help me determine right from wrong. The Book of Romans in the New Testament goes into great detail to explain the process, particularly chapters 3 through 8.

I have the example and the help of Christ himself. He understands me perfectly, and he has experienced temptation—without sinning (Hebrews 4:14–16). As I talk to him about my struggles, he promises to help me withstand temptation.

God has warned me about the consequences of my wrong thoughts and actions. He has given me good examples to follow and bad ones to avoid (Hebrews 12; 1 Corinthians 10:1–12). I may learn from both the good decisions and the mistakes of others.

Through the strength of other Christians, I can learn to stand against temptation. To stand alone sometimes seems impossible. But with the help of Christian friends, I gain great moral strength (Hebrews 10:24–25; James 5:16).

I am given a way to escape every temptation. First Corinthians 10:13 gives a remarkable promise: God will never allow me to be put in a situation of temptation that is too powerful for me. Always there is an escape. Usually I can see it clearly.

He paid for my sin and provides forgiveness based on his death and resurrection for me. There is always forgiveness and a new beginning (1 John 1:9).

Far from causing me to be tempted and to sin, God has done all this and more to help me rise above these problems.

Like Jeff, Brad, and Amy, I know how guilt feels. But like them also, I know how it feels to be forgiven. And though I often fail, I am doing better at finding that way of escape out of temptation. It seems hard to believe that God could love me this much. That he would forgive me so freely. That he would help me so patiently.

✓ Monday Checkpoint: *Temptation*

Sin is not just something I do, it is something I like to do.

☞ Think about it . . .

God, on the other hand, sees sin clearly for what it is, and he hates it for all it destroys. There is nothing in God that responds to sin and says, "Hmmm, nice stuff!"

So where did we get this inclination of ours?

We get angry, and for a while at least, we seem to enjoy the feeling. We may even find pleasure in hurting others, choosing mean words that will inflict pain. Or we pamper and feed our lust, as if those inappropriate sexual desires deserve our tender care. Or we gossip about others, tearing them down behind their backs, all the while finding some twisted pleasure in their misfortune.

It does not take a whole lot of honesty to admit we have a problem. For most of us, the truth is plain and unescapable. If we are ever to find a solution to all that is so wrong within us, it will have to come from something *outside* us. It will have to come from someone very much unlike us.

☞ God's Word says . . .

"When tempted, no one should say, 'God is tempting me.' For God cannot be tempted by evil, nor does he tempt anyone" (James 1:13).

☞ Make it a prayer . . .

Lord, you are all that I need. Thank you that you are so unlike me, yet have taken steps to make me so much like you.

Tuesday Checkpoint: *Temptation*

I feel it inside me, like bad gravity. A force which just keeps pulling me down.

Think about it . . .

Think about a temptation you have faced. Maybe it was impatience, anger. Maybe it was sexual. Maybe you wanted to put someone else down so you would feel better in the eyes of others—or in your own eyes.

In each of these examples, there is something *outside* us that is involved. We are angry because of something a parent has said, for instance, or a teacher or boss or friend. Something *made* us angry. We feel sexual temptation because of something we see or hear or feel. We gossip about someone because of something we saw or heard.

Because something outside us is so often involved in temptation, we may get the idea that temptation is something that is done *to* us, rather than something we do to ourselves. Something inside us. A problem with our own nature.

If I am going to deal with sin, I have to deal with *me.* Right now. Today.

God's Word says . . .

"Each one is tempted when, by his own evil desire, he is dragged away and enticed. Then, after desire has conceived, it gives birth to sin, and sin, when it is full grown, gives birth to death" (James 1:14–15).

Make it a prayer . . .

With your help, Lord, I will take responsibility for my actions today—and my thoughts, my words, my choices.

Wednesday Checkpoint: *Temptation*

There is nothing that sin can give me
that I truly need.

☞ Think about it ...

We have interesting ways of talking to ourselves. The songwriter says, "If it makes you happy, it can't be that bad." Look at it from one perspective and that makes some sense. But we are pretty tricky in the way we talk to ourselves. It is so easy for us to rationalize and make excuses for our mistakes and our sins.

We tell ourselves we had good reason to be angry, for instance. Or we experience intense pleasure and suddenly have little interest in listening to the voice of guilt. We can almost convince ourselves that we *needed* to sin. It was in our best interest. Remember the temptation of Adam and Eve? There was this idea that God was withholding something good from them. To get it, they would have to take it themselves. Now.

Isn't it fascinating, then, that as God talks to us about temptation, he also reminds us that he is the giver of all good gifts. God will meet our needs in legitimate ways. He will meet *all* of our needs in legitimate ways.

In other words, sin is unnecessary because God is so good.

☞ God's Word says ...

"Don't be deceived, my dear brothers. Every good and perfect gift is from above" (James 1:16–17).

☞ Make it a prayer ...

Thank you for your gifts, and the loving concern that prompts you to give.

Thursday Checkpoint: *Temptation*

Every temptation has a back door, or an open window. There is always a way of escape.

Think about it . . .

When I think back on ideas that have changed me and good news that has astounded me, I think immediately of this: *I will never face a temptation that is too strong for me. I will never encounter a temptation that does not have, built into it, a way of escape.*

Temptation can be unbelievably strong, but I don't have to yield. There is a way out. Always. Always. Always.

When I first read this good news, it stopped me. I could not keep reading. I had to pause and replay recent temptations and sins in my mind. I had lost my temper; I said things I deeply regretted. Did I have to? Was there a way of escape? At what point in the temptation could things have easily turned out differently?

I spent about a half hour thinking through various sins, replaying recent scenes from my memory. Over and over again, I could see the escape, and I knew it was true.

God's Word says . . .

"God is faithful; he will not let you be tempted beyond what you can bear. But when you are tempted, he will also provide a way out so that you can stand up under it" (1 Corinthians 10:13).

Make it a prayer . . .

Thank you, Lord, that there is always a way out. Make me want to take it.

Friday Checkpoint: *Temptation*

Do I really believe that God will make me clean? That I can stand next to him without embarrassment or shame?

☞ Think about it . . .

I had prayed before, and before that. I had asked forgiveness but fell to the same temptation once again. How could God forgive me for the same failure? Didn't he tire of my repeated apologies?

Here's a different way to think of it. It is the night before the death of Christ. He has already been betrayed, and he knows it. He will soon be arrested, but that will not surprise him. He will be dragged before the court and declared innocent and yet will be sentenced to death anyway. This too he sees in advance. It will be a slow, brutal execution, unimaginably painful. He knows. He has a clear picture of what the coming hours will bring.

But he also knows what this ordeal will achieve. He knows that as he dies, he will take the full penalty for the sins of the world—including your sins. Including the sins you will repeat over and over. Jesus sees it all in advance, yet he does not run away. He does not call for divine reinforcements. He does not turn against you. He goes ahead with the plan of God, in all its pain, and he does so willingly, lovingly, for you.

☞ God's Word says . . .

"If we confess our sins, he is faithful and just and will forgive us our sins and purify us from all unrighteousness" (1 John 1:9).

☞ Make it a prayer . . .

Thank you!

Week 3

Gratitude

James 1:16–18

Weekend Reading

Sometimes It's Hard to Say Thanks

> The truly important things in life are not things at all.

Dense fog squats above California's San Joaquin Valley, reducing visibility to near zero. And I stand, on a driveway in a small rural community forty-five miles northwest of Fresno, beneath the wet, gray underside of November.

At 7 A.M. life is already ruffling the fog's hazy tail feathers. Life stirs. An unseen screen door slams, a dog barks, and out of the mist, car headlights appear as two circles of diffused light. My hair is soaked from the moisture in the air, and I turn my collar against the chill.

Lifting the rear door of the beige VW van, a friend and I load the last of several corrugated boxes, then hop in. We have four stops to make this morning—food to distribute to four intensely needy families.

It is Thanksgiving, and gratitude is on my mind. But gratitude for what? That birth pushed me out into middle-class suburban life, instead of downward to the poverty I will witness this morning?

The VW creeps out of the driveway and down the street as we strain to define phantom shapes in the fog.

A left onto the east-west highway. Two miles. Right on the north-south. Five miles, I'd guess. Another right onto a gravel road that flanks the irrigation canal. After a few hundred yards we take a sharp left onto a muddy dirt road. Less than a mile and the van stops near a tree.

"We have a box for this family," my friend says.

"What family?" I squint into the flat gray and make out the shape of a crude lean-to of cardboard, chicken wire, and scrap lumber constructed around the base of a tree.

As I try to make sense out of what I am seeing, a grateful family, recognizing the van, emerges from this heap that is their home.

They, of course, are thankful to receive a box of food for the holiday. Profoundly so. They are smiling, laughing, chattering out their thanksgiving. But my mind is reeling. I feel a twinge of guilt over all I have compared to their little. I am embarrassed that such poverty exists, particularly in this country of such extravagance and wealth.

What is thanksgiving?

I've heard people trying to stir up thankfulness in others by quoting: "I complained that I had no shoes, until I met someone who had no feet." We could say it more pointedly, of course: "I complained that I had the wrong label on my athletic shoes, until I met someone with no legs."

But is this thanksgiving?

Okay, I see someone less fortunate. I'm glad I escaped his misfortune. This morning I am relieved that I sleep in a comfortable bed and live in my suburban home instead of a drafty lean-to at the edge of a field. But what then is supposed to motivate the homeless to thankfulness? Or the amputee? Who is there to inspire him to gratefulness? What's he supposed to tell himself? "I complained that I had no feet until . . . until what?"

I wonder: is it really gratitude if I'm just glad God "treated me better" than he treated these poor people? Is it really thankfulness if I'm just relieved that God didn't let *my* legs get cut off? Isn't there something more to gratitude than mere relief?

> *"Don't be deceived,"* the Bible tells me. *"Every good and perfect gift is from above, coming down from the Father of heavenly lights, who does not change like shifting shadows" (James 1:16–17).*

But how am I to react when the "gifts" life throws around are not good and perfect, but evil and imperfect?

I find it interesting that the Bible first says, "Do not be deceived," then says, "Every good and perfect gift is from above." The point, I take it, is this:

The good and perfect gifts are often surprises.

They do not necessarily come in expected ways. As I look at life—the disadvantaged, the amputee, my own down times—couldn't I conclude that there are no good gifts? No perfect gifts? No loving Giver? No strong God to be trusted?

But the verse says, "Don't be deceived."

Life can appear dismal, but is it possible that somewhere, in the worst of experiences, even there, God has wrapped a good and perfect gift, someday to be opened and revealed?

Don't be fooled.

Certainly this family, huddled around this tree, has a disproportionate share of disadvantages. Yet my friend tells me they get by without bitterness. Have they seen good and perfect gifts I have simply overlooked?

The gifts of God are good and perfect.

I take the words at face value. Much that God has given is unquestionably good and perfect. Gifts like friendship and love, taste and touch, sight and intelligence, hearing and smelling, beauty and wisdom, memory and forgetfulness.

But then I remember pain.

And yet even in pain, the words "good and perfect" come through to me.

> *"We know that in all things God works for the good of those who love him. . . . What, then, shall we say in response to this? If God is for us, who can be against us?" (Romans 8:28, 31).*

Good and perfect.

But the goodness and perfection may not show until later. Long after an uncomfortable wait.

The good gifts are from above, coming down.

I wonder why the stress on *above* and *coming down.* Is it because good and perfect gifts don't originate with Earth but have their source elsewhere?

"Set your minds on things above," the Bible tells me, "not on earthly things" (Colossians 3:2). The point: Earthly things can be disappointing.

I have heard that those who have little are often nevertheless joyful, thankful people. Those who have much lack gratitude and simply expect more.

Why?

Is it because some of us are "too blessed" to be thankful? We have too much. And our good stuff weighs us down, making it harder to think about the truly important things. The Bible gives us this riddle:

We are not to look at the things that are seen but at the things that are unseen. What is seen is temporary. What is unseen is eternal (2 Corinthians 4:18).

In thanksgiving, then, perspective is everything.

The truly important things are not "things" at all.

"Every good and perfect gift is *from above.*"

But are these "answers" enough?

Momentarily, I will be leaving this family in their cold and discomfort. Later today, I and fourteen other people will sit at a huge dining table and eat more than any of us needs. In the evening, we will relax together, comparatively carefree.

Meanwhile, what will this family do? They'll have this food they would not otherwise have had. But it will not last. In a few days, the menu will again become skimpy and bland. Can I imagine life from this family's perspective? How does it feel to be hungry? How do they react when they need clothes they cannot afford? What goes on inside this father's mind when his children are cold?

I have only fragmentary answers for the deep mysteries of want and pain. I do know these things are temporary—God will someday change them. I know that even now he reaches out to help us; he feels the want and pain with us. In the midst of the best and the worst of times, mysteriously, he gives. The gifts come down to us "from the Father of heavenly lights, who does not change like shifting shadows." (Sometimes he gives to others through me; he expects that of me.)

And then there's this thought: *"He chose to give us birth through the word of truth, that we might be a kind of firstfruits of all he created" (James 1:18).*

God has wrapped the future and presented it as a gift waiting to be opened.

My new life as a Christian—and yours—is God's guarantee that he will change for good the imperfect world that holds us captive to want and pain. As a kind of firstfruits of all he created, the change he has begun in us will spread to all creation. The shacks and hunger will be removed.

But the wait is so long.

The family turns toward their home, still looking back to wave. I call out a final holiday greeting, then slam the VW's lift gate.

A moment later the van rumbles to life and inches forward through the fog. Three more stops, then home for dinner.

Will the fog ever lift?

Monday Checkpoint: *Gratitude*

All around us, constantly, there are reasons to say, "Thanks!"

☞ Think about it . . .

Some things make me wonder. Why is it that sometimes people who have so little are truly grateful, while others who have so much just complain because they don't have more? What makes some people bitter and gloomy, and others appreciative and upbeat? Why must some people look at those who are less fortunate before they can stir up any feeling of thankfulness, while others face tough things in life, yet still feel that God is kind?

We feel thankful when we unexpectedly receive something good. We are all given excellent gifts every day—astoundingly good things—but because we *expect* them, it does not occur to us to be thankful.

For example, we have the gift of sight. We experience things that are beautiful, and we avoid catastrophe all because we can see. Very few of us would think to say thanks for such a remarkable gift, unless we were suddenly in danger of losing it. Or unless we met someone who did not have the gift. Then we remember.

God asks us to stop, to think about the wonders around us, and to remember to give thanks.

☞ God's Word says . . .

"Give thanks in all circumstances, for this is God's will for you in Christ Jesus" (1 Thessalonians 5:18).

☞ Make it a prayer . . .

Thank you, Lord, for sight and hearing, for taste and touch, for feeling and thought, for friends and family, and health and forgiveness.

Tuesday Checkpoint: *Gratitude*

Could it be that hidden behind every disappointment is a good gift waiting to be discovered?

☞ Think about it . . .

How am I supposed to react when life seems unfair? It seems crazy to say, "Thanks!"

God does not write us off because we are disappointed, or doubtful. We are warned about grumbling and complaining, and yet the Psalms often present human frustration and deep questions. The Psalms also are full of thanks. Time and time again complaint is turned to praise; questions are turned to gratitude; anxiety gives way to thanksgiving.

Here's what's weird about this: oftentimes the attitude changes long before the circumstances do. Life is still frightening or frustrating or unfair, but suddenly the perspective has shifted. Somewhere, behind the gloom, God is doing something, and because he is, people are thankful.

This is what we need: a new perspective. Life will bring its frustrations, but don't be fooled: God is alive and at work! Nothing will frustrate his good purpose.

☞ God's Word says . . .

"Don't be deceived. . . . Every good and perfect gift is from above, coming down from the Father of the heavenly lights, who does not change like shifting shadows" (James 1:16–17).

☞ Make it a prayer . . .

Thank you for your good gifts, especially those that may yet be hidden.

Wednesday Checkpoint: *Gratitude*

Life may give me troubles, but God's gifts are good and perfect.

Think about it . . .

The surgeon lifts his knife, lowers the blade, makes his incision, which is trailed by a red ribbon of blood. Were you not anesthetized, you would most certainly feel the pain. Tissue splits under the scalpel's razor edge. There is nothing natural about this experience. If we knew nothing of it, if we had no trust in medical procedure, we would be horrified. We walk into a brightly illuminated room. A sinister, masked figure hunches over a body. He is surrounded by accomplices as he bends to the task. You see the blood and realize with horror that he's slicing someone open. What good could possibly come of this?

Yet, knowing what we know, instead of being horrified, we are thankful. Instead of thinking the man a criminal, we find him good. What appears to be a game of death is instead an exercise in health. We know the man's purpose and we trust his skill.

What we observe has not changed, but the perspective has, and that makes all the difference. Is it really surprising, then, that God might be able to bring good out of circumstances that right now appear to be so bad?

God's Word says . . .

"We know that in all things God works for the good of those who love him. . . . What, then, shall we say in response to this? If God is for us, who can be against us?" (Romans 8:28, 31).

Make it a prayer . . .

Lord, your skill amazes me!

Thursday Checkpoint: *Gratitude*

There is a place to look when frustration comes. A way to turn when life is most confusing. Look up!

☞ Think about it . . .

This could sound trite, I suppose. Or could lead to a sore neck. But there really is some point to it.

James says, "Don't be deceived. Every good and perfect gift is from above, coming down from the Father." Look closer. What is he saying? Don't be deceived. Life is not what it appears to be. If you look at life and draw your conclusions too quickly, you might be fooled. You might think there are no good gifts, or you might mistake their origin.

Where do good gifts come from? James emphasizes the point. Good gifts, *perfect* gifts are *from above*, *coming down*—every one of them. The disappointing things are all around us, earthly. The good stuff is heavenly.

Look down, look around you, you will see frustration, disappointment, evil. You will see some good stuff too, but those good things did not originate here, they came down, from above. Good and perfect gifts from a Father who loves us.

☞ God's Word says . . .

"Set your minds on things above, not on earthly things" (Colossians 3:2).

☞ Make it a prayer . . .

Thank you, Father, that you care enough about what happens here, that you take your good gifts, and place them where we can reach them.

Friday Checkpoint: *Gratitude*

God's best gifts are wrapped in "forever," tied up with "tomorrow."

☞ Think about it . . .

God gives good gifts. Perfect gifts. But that does not mean he is satisfied with the pain we endure. Sometimes it is hard to say thanks. Sometimes we are trapped in circumstances that, frankly, stink. We may find reason for hope. We may even experience joy. But God does not expect us to be satisfied forever with crummy conditions.

In this world, we enjoy the gifts of God. But in this world, we also confront sadness, disappointment, sickness, and death. Relationships fall apart. Children go hungry. Accidents happen. People get violent. Bad news is not confined to news reports; it has the annoying ability also to become personal. Sometimes, that bad news creeps into *your* life.

Remember where good and perfect gifts come from? They are from above, coming down from the Father. If you want that which is good and perfect, sooner or later you must go where goodness and perfection originate. You must join them at their source. Above. In heaven. With the Father. And God gives us even this, his most perfect gift: eternal life.

And God gives us even this, his most perfect gift: eternal life.

☞ God's Word says . . .

"He chose to give us birth through the word of truth, that we might be a kind of firstfruits of all he created" (James 1:18).

☞ Make it a prayer . . .

Someday, I will see you and suddenly I will forget my pain. I will put my sadness behind me. I will be caught up in all that is truly good and perfect.

Week 4

True Faith

James 1:19–27

Weekend Reading

Doing the Right Thing

How is it that some people walk into the room and everything comes alive, sort of like a brief, spontaneous party?

My wife and I spent some time together yesterday. We had lunch, then took a few minutes to drive around and talk. No big agenda. Just a brief break from other responsibilities. I noticed something about being with her, something almost corny—like it could be engraved on a greeting card or something: that time together was a bright spot in my day.

Later that afternoon, I was thinking about the difference one person can make—in your day, yes, but maybe even in your whole life. I wasn't just thinking about people in whom you have a romantic interest. It could be a friend, an acquaintance, even a stranger, I suppose, who makes a difference.

Some people walk into the room and everything comes alive. Sort of like a brief, spontaneous party. Then there are those other people: when you see them coming, you want to hide. They walk into the room; the emotional lights dim and flicker.

I thought about the power of people off and on throughout the afternoon. In fact, by evening, I was feeling a bit philosophical. What is it about a person that impresses me? What qualities define the people who make a difference in my life? I decided to make a list (you might want to do the same). Here's what I came up with:

Sees good in others, and brings out the best in them.

Always has something positive to say.

Is there when I need someone.

Has a great sense of humor; lightens things up.

Is a good listener.

Cares about people and unselfishly helps them in practical ways.

Has strong convictions about things that truly matter.

I picked up this list of character traits, read it through a few times, and realized that though it wasn't exhaustive (there are other things that also matter), it was a sort of snapshot of what I want to be. A sketch of what matters. Being "truly religious" matters to me, and this list captured for me something of the daily difference true religion ought to make.

So what's hindering me?

Something to dig up. Something to plant.

"Take note of this: Everyone should be quick to listen, slow to speak and slow to become angry" (James 1:19).

If I pulled out another piece of paper and—even though it isn't as much fun—listed the kind of people I most want to avoid, I know who would top the list:

Angry people.

Critical people.

Negative people.

If I listed what I like least about me, it would be those times that I am critical, angry, negative.

There are other faults in the world—and in me—but the angry misuse of words makes my list because it is so destructive, yet so widespread. Fed by impatience and frustration, anger grows quickly. Words that cannot be taken back slip out so easily. And "man's anger does not bring about the righteous life that God desires" (James 1:20).

The life that *I* desire.

> *"Therefore, get rid of all moral filth and the evil that is so prevalent and humbly accept the word planted in you, which can save you" (James 1:21).*

If I am to cultivate the qualities in my first list (sensitivity, caring, listening), I must dig up and toss away my tendency toward careless words and angry reactions. This would seem impossible, except that something else has been planted in me: words from God that can change me.

But how do the changes come about?

It's more than listening.

It seems so obvious as to be silly, but for God's words to change me, I must first listen to them. What is not so obvious is that listening to them can deceive me if listening is all I do.

> *"Do not merely listen to the word, and so deceive yourselves. Do what it says" (James 1:22).*

I am not deceived if I do not listen—not in the same way, at least. But if I listen to God's words *without acting on them*, I am deceived. Why? Because I begin to think I am something special when I'm not. I go to church. I read the Bible. I listen to *Christian* music.

So what? Am I changed by all this I hear? Or am I merely fooling myself, thinking I'm something when I'm nothing?

> *"Anyone who listens to the word but does not do what it says is like a man who looks at his face in a mirror and, after looking at himself, goes away and immediately forgets what he looks like" (James 1:23–24).*

Think of it this way: if a mirror gives good news about you—if you are pleased with what you see—you are not as likely to want to forget. In fact, you may keep reminding yourself, pausing in front of every reflective surface you pass—store windows, shiny cars—admiring your image.

If the mirror gives you bad news—if you do not like your looks—you may want to forget.

Picturing the Bible as a mirror is interesting. In reading God's Book, I do get an accurate reflection of who I am. What I "look" like. What my weaknesses are. But this mirror has strange powers to change me, if only I will keep looking, rather than turning away discouraged.

"The man who looks intently into the perfect law that gives freedom, and continues to do this, not forgetting what he has heard, but doing it—he will be blessed in what he does" (James 1:25).

But what does this mean?

If I keep looking—listening—what will I become?

What will I "look like?"

The look of "true religion."

Well, first, what will I not look like?

"If anyone considers himself religious and yet does not keep a tight rein on his tongue, he deceives himself and his religion is worthless" (James 1:26).

I say that I do not like the company of critical people, angry people, negative people. I do not like it when I am critical, angry, negative. Well, if I let my words run wild in unkindness and anger, I am not truly the good person I say I want to be. If I say I am "religious" or "Christian," yet can control neither my temper nor my tongue, I'm just fooling myself.

"True religion" has a different, better look.

"Religion that God our Father accepts as pure and faultless is this: to look after orphans and widows in their distress and to keep oneself from being polluted by the world" (James 1:27).

It is a rather amazing statement that God can accept my "religion" as pure and faultless. But it is not measured by the words I read, the sermons I endure, the

Christian concerts I attend, the Bible-verse T-shirts I put on. It is measured by what I do.

And what am I to do?

I am to keep myself from being polluted by the world. This challenges how I think and live. What I watch and read and hear.

But I also take special care of those in need. "Widows" and "orphans." People who have lost what matters to them most. People who are lonely and neglected. People who are not in the inner circle of popularity and attention.

I ask myself, what will I look like to them? When I walk into the room, will I make a difference in their lives?

I glance again at my list of qualities I appreciate in others. Would the "neglected people" I touch—as well as my friends—describe me like this?

> Sees good in others, and brings out the best in them.
>
> Always has something positive to say.
>
> Is there when I need someone.
>
> Has a great sense of humor; lightens things up.
>
> Makes me want to be a better person.
>
> Is a good listener.
>
> Cares about people and unselfishly helps them in practical ways.
>
> Has strong convictions about things that truly matter.

For me, today, this is a measure of "true religion."

Monday Checkpoint: *True Faith*

One person can make a difference in the world. And that one person could be you.

Think about it ...

We all know people who have changed us in some way, people who have somehow impressed us and brought out the best in us. If you were to make a list right now of the people who have had the biggest impact on you, who would make the list? A friend? A parent? An aunt or uncle? A teacher, a boss, a youth leader?

Think about a person who has changed you, someone who has made you a better person. What were they like? What was it about them that left an impression on you? How would you describe that person?

My guess is, you would not describe that person as mean, spiteful, negative, boring, self-centered, dishonest. When we describe people who have transformed us, people who have made us better, most of us tend to come up with words like these: kind, upbeat, unselfish, honest, caring.

It kind of makes you wonder: what impact might you have if those words described you? One person *can* make a difference in the world. And that one person *can* be you.

God's Word says ...

"Do not merely listen to the word, and so deceive yourselves. Do what it says" (James 1:22).

Make it a prayer ...

Lord, please make a difference in me, so that I will make a difference in others.

Tuesday Checkpoint: *True Faith*

What would you do if you looked deep down inside yourself and found something there that was hurting you?

Think about it ...

Just as certainly as some people are pleasant to be around, others are annoying. You see them coming, you head the other way, avoiding them at all cost. Your list is probably similar to mine. The people I most want to avoid are angry people, critical people, negative people.

If I want to be a person who makes a difference in the world, a person who brings out the best in others, I must take an honest look at myself. What about my anger? My criticism? My grumbling?

If you were to skim the book of James, there are certain ideas you would immediately notice. Things that concern the writer. One of them is our careless use of words. When James says, "Get rid of all moral filth," I may convince myself he's talking about someone else. When I listen to my words, I can no longer argue. I am sinful. I do have stuff I must dig up and throw away. There are things inside that hurt me. Why keep them another minute?

God's Word says ...

"Get rid of all moral filth and the evil that is so prevalent and humbly accept the word planted in you, which can save you" (James 1:21).

Make it a prayer ...

Without your help, I could never change. With your help, I can change even the world.

Wednesday Checkpoint: *True Faith*

God's words can change you, and the change will be wonderful. Now what?

Think about it . . .

You realize you are ill. Your stomach is churning, your head is throbbing, your eyes hurt. Your shivering convinces you of your fever. You are weak and light-headed, and the symptoms persist. By the time you make it to the doctor, you are genuinely concerned—a concern you see mirrored on his face. But he reassures you, gives you an accurate diagnosis, stuffs a prescription in your hand. You leave his office knowing that your restored health is as simple as following a few instructions, and being patient with the healing process.

Upon returning home, you put the medication aside, unopened. You disregard the instructions to force liquids and get plenty of rest. Not surprisingly, your health fails to improve; if anything, it worsens. At times, this concerns you—so much so, that you take out the medication and the doctor's instructions and spend a few minutes looking at them. Nevertheless, looking at them is as far as it goes.

Now, what's wrong with this picture?

God's Word says . . .

"Anyone who listens to the word but does not do what it says is like a man who looks at his face in a mirror and, after looking at himself, goes away and immediately forgets what he looks like" (James 1:23–24).

Make it a prayer . . .

Motivate me to act on what I know to be true!

Thursday Checkpoint: *True Faith*

If we could see ourselves as we really are, we might be tempted to run away and hide.

☞ Think about it . . .

But hope for change begins with that true picture—who we are, what we can become.

The Bible is a mirror. It gives an accurate reflection of who we are. It shows us what is inside us. If we don't like what we see, it is natural to draw back, to want to look elsewhere. But this is no ordinary mirror. This mirror not only shows us what we are, it shows us what we can become. More than this even, looking into this mirror is a transforming experience. Under its power we become new.

Think back over your own experience. What has your faith taught you about yourself? How has it already changed you? In what ways have you become a better person because God is alive and active within you?

Look in the mirror. What great changes now await you?

☞ God's Word says . . .

"The man who looks intently into the perfect law that gives freedom, and continues to do this, not forgetting what he has heard, but doing it—he will be blessed in what he does" (James 1:25).

☞ Make it a prayer . . .

Thank you, Father, that you love so much that you will not rest until I am the person you want me to become.

Friday Checkpoint: *True Faith*

You have the power to put a smile on God's face. Want to know how?

☞ Think about it . . .

It's truly remarkable to think that God could look at us and be pleased by what he sees. We know our weaknesses; *he* knows them in infinitely greater detail. How can we please God? When he looks at us, what could he possibly see that would put a smile on his face?

You may already know. Complete this phrase: "God would be pleased if I were less . . ." Less what? What is there in your life today that should not be there?

Try this. "God would be pleased if I were more . . ." More what? What are the good things about you that ought to increase?

When we read Scripture and listen to our conscience, we get an accurate image of what we are; a clear reflection of what we can become. That mirror only fogs over when we are hypocritical, when we tell ourselves how good we are, yet go on hurting others and hurting ourselves.

☞ God's Word says . . .

"Religion that God our Father accepts as pure and faultless is this: to look after orphans and widows in their distress and to keep oneself from being polluted by the world" (James 1:27).

☞ Make it a prayer . . .

Give me a great and unselfish concern for people who are lonely and neglected—people who are not in the inner circle of popularity and attention. And give me a deep desire to be truly good.

Week 5

Favoritism

James 2:1–13

Weekend Reading

Playing Favorites

When I look at the crowd, is that all I see?
Or are there people behind those faces?

It begins first thing in the morning. You get up, prepare yourself for the day and, most likely, say good-bye to a family member or two before facing the outside world. But when you pass your father or mother, brother or sister—or when you sit across the breakfast table from them—what do you see?

You leave the house on your way to school. You get on a crowded bus or pass others walking or pull your car into a congested parking lot. Everywhere there are people—short, tall; fat, thin; plain, attractive; Hispanic, Norwegian. When you see them, what do you think?

You walk down hallways traffic-jammed with students. You sit for hours in desk-crammed rooms with twenty or thirty others. You move toward the cafeteria through tight knots of people. You take your place in a long line and look for an empty space amid a sea of faces. When you glance around the room at all these people—people like you and unlike you—what comes to mind?

One day passes. How many faces have you seen? What impression has it all made?

People labels: designer, generic.

Maybe it is because we face so many human beings in a day that we are driven to label them and put them into categories. Maybe it is because we are lazy or fearful that we keep them there.

Brains and burn-outs.

Jocks and geeks.

Designer labels and generic labels.

As soon as we paste on a label, we don't have to treat the person so much like a person. They've become, instead, a category.

In a sense, we even do this with family. I label my brother or my mother as family, then go on to take him or her for granted. If I treated a friend the way I often treat my mother, would the friendship survive?

We also label and categorize ourselves into friendship groups. While it may be unspoken, we know the designer group that makes us most comfortable. No wonder we rarely get to know people who are in some other "category"—people who are different from us.

Before long, we have our world neatly divided between the people who impress us, to whom we give designer labels, and those we dislike or overlook, whom we consider generic.

The unfortunate result: we look at a crowd and see a crowd; rarely do we catch a glimpse of *individuals* with feelings, struggles, disappointments, ideas, potential. Rarely do we look beyond the exterior that either impressed us or repelled us, long enough to see the true person inside.

The problem with playing favorites.

I was reading the New Testament book of James, which talks about how terrifying favoritism is, and was suddenly impressed with the problem. Most of us hate racial discrimination, even if we have our own tenacious prejudices to contend with. We see the evil and hurt that come from putting negative labels on people. But do we see the problem with *favoritism*? Do we see that it is merely another face on discrimination?

Attacking those we do not like, based solely on the label we give them, is prejudice in action. Heaping advantages on those we *do* like and are trying to impress is favoritism.

The two are really flip sides of the same coin. Favoritism, like prejudice, is an attack on those we don't like—those who do not measure up to our good labels. It is just a sneak attack from behind. A roundabout road to prejudice.

The Bible condemns it, and for good reason.

When I practice favoritism, I become an evil judge.

When I sort people by designer labels and generic labels, and treat them differently based on looks or race or social background, I am setting myself up as judge. But I am judging by poor and unfair standards. What good judge would disregard the evidence in favor of how the defendant dressed? What good judge would put reason aside and hand down the strictest of consequences, all based on racial differences?

Don't we do the same thing in our "small" way when we exclude some people and favor others based on externals like race or intelligence or looks?

> *"As believers in our glorious Lord Jesus Christ, don't show favoritism" (James 2:1).*

The writer illustrates: Two people arrive at your meeting at the same time. One is obviously rich, the other poor. There are only a few seats left. How do you decide who sits where? Who gets the place of honor? Suppose you give the good seat to the rich guy, then say to the tramp, "Sit on the floor by my feet" (2:2–3).

> *"Have you not discriminated among yourselves and become judges with evil thoughts?" (James 2:4).*

How do I decide who will be my friend? Who will be invited to the meeting? Or the party? Who is "in," who is "out?"

Favoritism shows I have wrong values.

When I pass judgment based on labels and categories, I put myself in conflict with God, who treats people as people. Who sees beyond appearance. Who knows what people think and how they feel.

But even if we were to place people in categories, aren't there "categories" that deserve our careful attention?

Yes.

The poor. The lonely. The neglected.

It's not that we are to give them special attention because of their "label" but because of their experience and their need. It's not wrong to be a friend to the popular and powerful people, but why should I begin with them when there are others who have been hurt, neglected, and disregarded?

The Bible writer complained because people were catering to the rich, even though the rich had oppressed them (2:5–7). As they were running after the approval of the popular, they disregarded the poor all around them. This is still wrong, whether big religious groups do it or whether we do it individually.

> *"Has not God chosen those who are poor in the eyes of the world to be rich in faith?" (James 2:5).*

When I play favorites, I break the law of God.

How seriously does God take this? Read his concern:

> *"If you really keep the royal law found in Scripture, 'Love your neighbor as yourself,' you are doing right. But if you show favoritism, you sin and are convicted by the law as lawbreakers" (James 2:8).*

God's law is like a chain, consisting of many links. To break any one principle is to break the chain (2:9–11). Murder breaks the chain. So does sexual sin. Two examples James gives. We look at the Big Sins and see their damage. But partiality breaks the chain too—favoritism and prejudice. In fact, if you were to summarize the law—if you were to give a simple principle or two, rather than listing all of the specifics—this would be it: "Love the Lord, and love people."

Excluding people by playing favorites is hateful.

Not loving.

Tearing off the labels.

So how is favoritism overcome? How can we break the pattern?

Live the law of God. As I let God's values—what he considers important—direct me, I will see people differently. I will treat them like people, regardless of the labels and categories that have been unfairly slapped on them.

It helps to remember that God is the true judge, and he judges by fair standards. He extends mercy and forgiveness where it is most needed and least deserved.

> *"Speak and act as those who are going to be judged by the law that gives freedom, because judgment without mercy will be shown to anyone who has not been merciful. Mercy triumphs over judgment!" (James 2:12–13).*

God considers people important. He places value on them. *Individually.*

Particularly the poor, the lonely, the forgotten.

This means I must begin to see the crowd differently. I must stop being impressed by things that do not matter—money, the right clothes, the right neighborhood. Instead, I must see people *as people* who often need a word of friendship, an expression of kindness, the gift of being included.

After all, on the one hand you could say that we are all rather generic, with our flaws and faults. That ought to make us tolerant, understanding, and forgiving.

On the other hand, we are all Designer-made, with such unimaginable value that God himself would pay the ultimate price for us. That ought to be so humbling that we put prejudice and favoritism behind us. Forever.

Monday Checkpoint: *Favoritism*

What happens when I label you or you label me?

Think about it . . .

In your mind, replay a typical day, from the moment you wake until, hours later, you lie down at night. How many people have you seen *in person*? Family and friends, yes, but also acquaintances and strangers. How many people have crossed your path, entered your vision? Add in television, movies, magazines. Can you even guess at a number?

Of all those people who crossed your path, how many did you *see*? How many were truly *individual* to you? And what of the others? We encounter so many people, we have little choice but to "see" them as nameless and faceless. A crowd. If we must deal with them at all, we tend to sort them and shuffle them into categories.

Now, look at yourself from the perspective of one of those nameless, faceless strangers. How many people saw you today, without really *seeing* you? Of those who saw you, how many sorted *you*, shuffled *you* into a category, then dismissed you from their mind?

It may be impossible to give everyone we see individual attention, but the Bible warns us against sorting "unseen" people into categories, then treating them differently because of it, showing prejudice or favoritism.

God's Word says . . .

"As believers in our glorious Lord Jesus Christ, don't show favoritism" (James 2:1).

Make it a prayer . . .

Help me see people as you see them, Lord.

Tuesday Checkpoint: *Favoritism*

How do I decide who will be my friend?
And how do I choose whom I will ignore?

☞ Think about it . . .

We are like judges. Each day we make hundreds of decisions; we weigh "evidence" and reach verdicts. We render judgments. Most of these decisions are mundane, trivial choices. But not all of them. When our choices involve others, how do we process the information? How do we make our decisions? How do we come to our conclusions? Are we honest, impartial judges? Or are we biased, swayed one way or another by unfair impressions?

The book of James gives this example. Two people come to your church—one nicely dressed, obviously wealthy; the other has the look of the homeless about him. What you do next—how you treat these two individuals—shows what kind of "judge" you are. Does the rich guy get special, favorable treatment? Do you push the homeless person aside, silently hoping he'll go away, that his looks or smell will not distract you from more pleasant thoughts?

Forget the outward things. Put aside the labels. See an individual, with individual needs, hopes, concerns, dreams. To do less is to be an evil judge.

☞ God's Word says . . .

"[If you show favoritism] have you not discriminated among yourselves and become judges with evil thoughts?" (James 2:4).

☞ Make it a prayer . . .

When it comes to my friends and acquaintances—or the strangers I see—what kind of judge am I?

Wednesday Checkpoint: *Favoritism*

When God looks at this crush of humanity, what does he see?

Think about it . . .

I remember Bill, because everybody wanted to be his friend. I remember Harold, because almost no one was his friend. I remember Bill, standing on the sidelines of a game, people crowded around him as he laughed and talked. I remember Harold, sitting alone in a long, deserted hallway during lunch.

I knew them both. Bill was not spoiled by popularity, Harold was not weird. He was, in fact, kind and likable. Who can explain the twists and turns of popularity?

You would not fault anyone for wanting to be Bill's friend, but in my mind I still see a long, lonely hallway and one sitting figure, bent over his lunch, completely alone.

God does not play favorites with us, but if there is a "category" that gets his particular attention, I think I know what it is. When he looks down on this crush of humanity, don't you think he looks on with special concern for those who are lonely or neglected? And don't you suppose that is a special concern he would have us share?

God's Word says . . .

"Has not God chosen those who are poor in the eyes of the world to be rich in faith?" (James 2:5).

Make it a prayer . . .

Lord, make me unselfish in my friendships, not just looking for what I can get out of it, but what I can contribute.

Thursday Checkpoint: *Favoritism*

What if we turned the law around: "Love yourself, as you love your neighbor"? What if I treated *me,* the way I treat you?

☞ Think about it . . .

Let's expand on this test, this personal inventory.

What if I treated my best friend the way I treat my father?

What if I treated my sister the way I treat a stranger?

What if I treated my enemies the way I treat my friends?

What if I treated a stranger the way I want to be treated?

What if I treated the "losers" the way I treat the popular people?

What if I looked at people and saw individuals who needed my concern?

The law of God is summarized in the expectation, "Love your neighbor as yourself." This means that we are to have an unselfish care for anyone in need. If prejudice leads me to ignore someone in need, to treat them as less than a neighbor, I am breaking the law of God. If I show favoritism to some and ignore others, I am breaking the law of God.

☞ God's Word says . . .

"If you really keep the royal law found in Scripture, 'Love your neighbor as yourself,' you are doing right. But if you show favoritism, you sin and are convicted by the law as lawbreakers" (James 2:8).

☞ Make it a prayer . . .

Teach me what it means to love without prejudice, favoritism, self-centeredness.

Friday Checkpoint: *Favoritism*

One day I looked at the crowd and saw beyond the blur.

Think about it . . .

I stepped off the plane, walked down the jetway, entered the terminal, caught up in the crowd. The voices around me rose in an unintelligible roar. No one was speaking English. Were it not for international symbols, the signs around me would be meaningless, incomprehensible. For some reason I paused. I looked into the faces of passers-by. I listened to their speech, heard their laughter. For one brief moment, behind their eyes, I caught a glimpse of soul. In this airport, in all this clamor of humanity, there is not a single individual unknown and unloved by God.

I board a bus, enter a subway, cross the mall, step into a classroom, walk up to the counter at McDonald's, cross the path of an old enemy, greet my sister, embrace my wife—I will never encounter another human being who is loved any less or any more by the God I call my friend.

Anything less than kindness is not enough. Anything mean-spirited will disappoint my Father, who loves individuals—and loves them unconditionally.

God's Word says . . .

"Speak and act as those who are going to be judged by the law that gives freedom, because judgment without mercy will be shown to anyone who has not been merciful. Mercy triumphs over judgment" (James 2:12–13).

Make it a prayer . . .

Father, help me to live as you live and see as you see.

Week 6

Hypocrisy

James 2:14–26

Weekend Reading

How Not to Be a Hypocrite

How can you criticize someone for being angry at religious people who fail to act on their faith?

Beneath me, the Pacific breakers roll in, crashing against the pilings of the Seal Beach pier and filling the air with the smell and taste of salt. Around me, down and to my right, hundreds of people soak up the sun's rays or splash in the cool surf. Noise and action are everywhere—except here, in front of me. I look into the eyes of a man, a stranger, almost old enough to be my grandfather. His face lobster-red. His hair gray, tousled by the wind. His eyes squinting against the mid-afternoon sun. His voice low and gruff.

I am here, talking to this man, because I decided to find people with time on their hands, people who might listen to my concerns.

The conversation is Jesus.

I am scared and feel awkward. It hardly seems natural to walk up to a perfect stranger and tell him your life story or to pry into his life, looking to see if he has room in there for Jesus. Yet, convinced that what I believe is true, it seems more frightening, awkward, and unnatural to keep Jesus to myself.

I am surprised that more than half the people I approach talk willingly. One person out of every eight or ten seems very interested, as if in interrupting them I have done them a favor.

My confidence bolstered, I approached the older red-faced man. At first, he was appreciative. Someone had shown interest in him, had cared enough to talk. Now, as the conversation unfolds, he senses my religious agenda. His mood shifts. He becomes harsh, raising his voice, and turning on me in anger.

Watching his face harden, I shift mental gears. I am now on the defensive—not listening, but calculating how I will counter his arguments. Until something he says stops me, forcing me, finally, to listen.

"My wife and I were active in church years ago," he tells me. "The pastor and the other church leaders were often in our home, and we were in theirs. Our closest friends were the church people. Then, quite suddenly, my wife became sick, and I guess they didn't know how to respond to that. It became difficult for her to get out, so I stayed home to help her. As she grew worse, I became lonely and depressed. One day I realized it had been a long time since we had heard from the church. Nobody visited, nobody called, nobody wrote. Then one day my wife died, and the church sent flowers!"

Emotion chokes the man as he relives his sorrow and anger and disappointment. What am I to say?

I know that the hypocrisy of church people is a common argument against faith. People hide behind the hypocrites. I could say, "You have to be smaller than something to hide behind it." I could say, "A fake is just a copy of the real thing. An imitation Christian just shows there is something genuine to imitate." But the canned comebacks are hollow and stupid. The man has a point.

Faith without action is not faith.

I remember feeling relieved when I read the New Testament and found that it criticized hypocrisy. It felt as if God was agreeing with me: "You're right, Jim, hypocrisy is ugly." I had not yet got to the point of recognizing and admitting my own inconsistencies, but I detested the quality in others.

And I considered: *What if God did not criticize hypocrisy? What if he acted as if nothing was wrong?* I'm not sure I could have continued in my faith. Instead, I read words such as these:

> *"What good is it, my brothers, if a man claims to have faith but has no deeds? Can such faith save him? Suppose a brother or sister is without clothes and daily food. If one of you says to him, 'Go, I wish you well; keep warm and well fed,' but does nothing about his physical needs, what good is it? In the same way, faith by itself, if it is not accompanied by action, is dead" (James 2:14–17).*

If you refuse to be with someone in their need, don't insult them by later sending flowers.

Action demonstrates faith.

The flip side of the hypocrisy point is this: *It is action that proves faith.* What's on the inside will show on the outside.

Some people will try to argue that faith and action can be separated. That you can have faith without it showing itself, or you can have action without faith. *"You have faith; I have deeds" (2:18).* But the Bible insists that faith is more—far more—than something we simply say.

> *"Show me your faith without deeds and I will show you my faith by what I do. You believe that there is one God. Good! Even the demons believe that—and shudder" (James 2:18–19).*

To put it another way, faith does not come to life until it is acted upon. It is useless until it expresses itself. Until I break from my hypocrisy, my God-talk means nothing.

For example:

> *"You foolish man, do you want evidence that faith without deeds is useless?" (James 2:20).*

With that introduction, the Bible gives two examples. The example of a good, religious man, Abraham, who proved his faith by *doing something* (2:21–23), and the example of a prostitute who changed her ways by finding a faith that was more than mere talk (2:25).

> *"You see that [Abraham's] faith and his actions were working together, and his faith was made complete*

by what he did. . . . A person is justified by what he does and not by faith alone. . . . As the body without the spirit is dead, so faith without deeds is dead" (James 2:22, 24, 26).

With words like these in the Bible, it is difficult to criticize a man who is confused, angry, and disappointed by religious people who fail to act on their faith.

I remember my early experiences with Christianity. I remember how I felt when I found out that my favorite Sunday school teacher left his wife and kids to run off with some other woman. I remember the business-meeting fights in my small church. I remember the deep disappointment I felt in myself when my actions and my words of faith conflicted—those times when I too was the hypocrite.

My mood shifts, as the older man's mood had shifted. I share his anger, his disappointment, even his sorrow.

Our eyes meet as he repeats himself, shaking his head: "The church sent flowers! Where were they when we needed them?"

The question hangs in the air. For a moment we are both quiet. When I finally find words to say, it is nothing profound or convincing, because it is rarely words alone that convince, but actions.

"I don't know," I tell the man, and we are both silent again. For a moment he just looks at me, then he turns to walk away. I stand there, watching until he disappears into the crowd.

Over the past ten or fifteen minutes, nothing has changed. The breakers are still rolling in, that salt-smell still fills the air, the crowd is still carefree. But inside me, much has changed. I find myself looking at the people around me on the pier and on the beach below, wondering what hurt and disappointment they may be carrying with them, under the surface.

More than that, I am shaken. I will never forget the pain I saw on that man's face. I will remember it often, especially when I am tempted to say I believe and yet am unwilling to prove it by how I live.

Monday Checkpoint: Hypocrisy

What happens when I *say* one thing, and *do* another?

Think about it . . .

You awaken and go through your routine, preparing for the day. You're going to school, you're not going to wear a formal. You have a basketball game, you're not likely to hit the floor in a band uniform. You're going to work, so you grab that funny-looking vest and hat; it's part of the job. You're expected to fit in. We are well skilled at adapting to our surroundings, chameleon-like, and fitting in.

When we're around certain of our friends, we may not only dress like them, we also talk like them and act like them. Then, with our church friends, we adapt again. Perhaps the language changes. Then, we're home, in yet another environment. Words we freely use around our friends are not spoken in front of mom.

Fitting in is one thing; hypocrisy quite another—and we understand them both.

At some point in life, our values become so much a part of us that instead of just conforming to what's *around us*, we conform to those beliefs that are *within us*. When that happens consistently, we leave hypocrisy behind.

God's Word says . . .

"Faith by itself, if it is not accompanied by action, is dead" (James 2:17).

Make it a prayer . . .

Lord, help me live as I believe. Make my actions consistent with my faith. Mold my life around my deepest beliefs.

Tuesday Checkpoint: *Hypocrisy*

What is on the *inside* will show on the *outside*. Now, how does that make you feel? Encouraged? Or nervous?

☞ Think about it . . .

The preacher gave intelligent talks, which was fine. But not always easy to listen to. Just seeing him up front preaching, it was easy to form an unflattering opinion of him. BOR-ING. Then I took a 300-mile trip with him; he took me to a camp high in California's Sierra Nevada. I made a discovery. The man was hilarious. And he was kind. Before, I saw him merely as a suit, stuffed with a talking mannequin—a plastic dummy with a good vocabulary. Now, I saw him as a *person*; and more than a person, I saw him as a friend.

The better I got to know my preacher friend, the more I saw that his life matched his beliefs. At church, you can be a fake, but spend enough time with someone, and the real person will show up, sooner or later.

What if we had taken that trip and I had discovered he was phony, a cheap imitation Christian? I would have left the church. Instead, I decided I wanted to be like him.

☞ God's Word says . . .

"What good is it, my brothers, if a man claims to have faith but has no deeds? Can such faith save him?" (James 2:14).

☞ Make it a prayer . . .

Lord, I don't want to be a cheap, imitation Christian. When someone spends time with me, help them see a real faith.

Wednesday Checkpoint: *Hypocrisy*

Want to know if your faith is real? Try this simple test.

☞ Think about it . . .

Don't ask yourself: What do I *believe*?

Don't ask yourself: What do I *say* I believe?

Ask yourself: What do I *do*?

True faith expresses itself in action. It does good stuff.

I sat in Chemistry class and heard about some experiment we were supposed to do. Combine this powder with that fluid, and there will be a reaction—smoke and color and a bit of a stink. I don't remember what we were trying to prove, but I do remember standing at the counter with my lab partner. I remember the beaker and the flame. I remember how we smiled and winked and nodded knowingly as we decided to double all the ingredients. And I very distinctly recall that nothing happened.

Well, nothing happened *until* we tossed all those ingredients together. Then, we woke up the class.

It's similar with faith. True faith is a catalyst. When it's present in your life, people are going to know it. There will be a display. Your life will be different.

☞ God's Word says . . .

"Show me your faith without deeds, and I will show you my faith by what I do. You believe that there is one God. Good! Even the demons believe that—and shudder" (James 2:18–19).

☞ Make it a prayer . . .

Give me a faith that proves itself in action.

Thursday Checkpoint: *Hypocrisy*

God likes to collect examples. Good examples. Want to be one of them? Here's how.

☞ Think about it . . .

Suppose God wanted to change the world, how would he do it? Would he write a message in the clouds? Would he miraculously appear at the United Nations General Assembly? Would he accept a guest appearance on late night TV? Or would he work through people? People who lived a genuine faith.

Think about all those Bible stories you've heard. When God wanted to change the world, how did he do it? He worked through individuals. Abraham, Moses, Rahab, David, Gideon, Ruth, Mary, John, Paul. Some of the people he used might seem to be unlikely candidates—a murderer, a prostitute, a timid geek. But he worked through all kinds of people, changing them and using them to change others.

Now, suppose God wanted to change *your* world? Your family, your neighborhood, your school. How would he do it? Who would he use? All he needs is someone with genuine faith. Want the job?

☞ God's Word says . . .

"You see that [Abraham's] faith and his actions were working together, and his faith was made complete by what he did" (James 2:22).

☞ Make it a prayer . . .

Lord, it would be easy to set my goals too low. To get the silly idea that my one life does not make a difference, when all the while you might want to change the world through me.

Friday Checkpoint: *Hypocrisy*

I'm thinking of a number between "one" and "two."

Think about it . . .

When someone's hypocritical, we say he's "two-faced." But really now, at one time or another, aren't we all two-faced? We are not free from some lapse into hypocrisy. We are not all we want to be.

But neither are we all we *can* be—all we *will* be.

I met a man on a pier, and he was bitter. A church had failed him, and he could not forget. I remember him now not because I want to criticize his church or find fault with him but because I want to remind myself that one life can make a difference.

I was in grade school when my favorite Sunday school teacher disappeared. His absence had to be explained somehow, and so I learned that he had left his wife and family for another woman. That was years ago. Perhaps he has sought forgiveness and returned to faith. I do not know. But he comes to mind now because I don't want to forget: for good or for bad, one life can make a difference.

I will not settle for casual faith.

I will not settle for ordinary Christianity.

I want to be real.

God's Word says . . .

"As the body without the spirit is dead, so faith without deeds is dead" (James 2:26).

Make it a prayer . . .

Father, make me real. Don't let me ever become someone's excuse for not believing.

Week 7

Words

James 3:1–12

Weekend Reading

The Power of All Our Talk

Our words don't have to tear people down. They also have the power to help.

You hardly would have noticed him, slouched in his seat, embarrassed and humiliated. What drew my attention to him as I boarded the bus was that four or five guys in the back were harassing him—throwing things at him, calling him names, for no apparent reason. They figured he looked funny, I guess. He didn't even turn around; just sank a bit lower in the green vinyl seat.

I took one of the few remaining places, across the aisle and two rows in front of the guy. The bus pulled away from the curb, and the ridicule continued, louder and more abusive. Along with the guys in the back of the bus, another stray voice here or there would chime in, all focused on this one individual.

I glanced at him over my shoulder. He sat there, hunched over and slump-shouldered, staring at the back of the seat in front of him, trying, I am sure, to block out all those voices. He did look kind of funny. He was pale, and his face and neck were marked with severe acne. He wore a bulky olive-green windbreaker, snapped shut all the way up, which made him look like a turtle with his neck extended out of the shell.

The bus was quiet for a moment, and then, in that comparative stillness, somebody came up with a new name. "Hey, Nerd Neck!" The back of the bus erupted in laughter. The name struck me funny, and I turned around, laughing with them. By now it seemed like everyone was taunting him, and I heard my own voice saying, "Hey, what's happenin', Nerd Neck?" He looked up and our eyes met. I felt like a total idiot. But how do you admit that?

A few minutes later the bus pulled up at the school. I grabbed my books and started across the parking lot. Immediately, I heard determined footsteps behind me and turned to see him heading my way—angry. Now that he was no longer slouched in the seat, I realized that he was bigger than I had thought. Bigger than I was, in fact. I realized, too, what was happening. Since he could not single-handedly go after the four or five guys in the back of the bus, he was bringing his frustration and fury to me.

The next few minutes blurred in a frenzy of motion and flailing fists. And pain. His ring opened my upper lip; blood was everywhere.

An hour later, I leaned back on the examining table as my doctor stitched the lip, which looked—and felt—like an inflated party balloon. Even then, sore as I was, I couldn't help feeling that on a small scale, justice had been done. It was my mouth, after all, that got me into trouble.

Our words measure us.

Time has passed. Yet I have often replayed that morning. When I do, I do not focus on this terrible guy who smashed his fist into my face. Instead, I see myself, grossly insensitive. I see myself hurting him. I am convinced that our words measure us. And my words that morning said how small I was.

> *"We all stumble in many ways. If anyone is never at fault in what he says, he is a perfect man, able to keep his whole body in check" (James 3:2).*

Our words are so important that the Bible even warns would-be teachers—people who intend to use words in *positive* ways—that they might want to think twice: those who teach "will be judged more strictly" (James 3:1). The more you use your voice, it would seem, the greater the risks. If we want to know what we're really like, all we need to do is listen to ourselves long enough.

So much from so little.

One hour ago I made an offhanded comment I didn't even mean. But I listened to my own words and heard unkindness. It seemed like such a small thing—careless words roll off the tongue effortlessly.

I am angry at my brother, so I pull out my arsenal of words; I say something that will hurt. Something he may, in fact, never forget. I disagree with my dad—a teacher or a boss. And I let them know, unmistakably. I punctuate my point with strong words. It is so easy. But so damaging.

> *"When we put bits into the mouths of horses to make them obey us, we can turn the whole animal. Or take ships as an example. Although they are so large and are driven by strong winds, they are steered by a very small rudder wherever the pilot wants to go. Likewise the tongue is a small part of the body, but it makes great boasts. Consider what a great forest is set on fire by a small spark" (James 3:3–5).*

If we want to know how powerful words are, all we have to do is remember. Remember the times we have been criticized, ridiculed, told we would fail. Remember the times words have hurt us. Remember the times we have been encouraged, praised, told we were certain to succeed. Remember the times words have helped us.

Words as weapons. Words as comfort.

When I am most honest with myself, I realize that I do not use words constructively nearly enough. I have scarcely tapped their power to help. It is so much easier to use them carelessly. To employ them to damage.

> *"The tongue is a fire, a world of evil among the parts of the body. It corrupts the whole person, sets the whole course of his life on fire, and is itself set on fire by hell" (James 3:6).*

How savage can our words become? Well, if we want to know what hell is like, all we have to do is listen to ourselves during our worst moments of verbal abuse. There is a window on the fires of hell, and that window is our destructive words.

Tough to tame.

Words can also be a window on heaven. They can frame and showcase all that is good. But it is not easy for me to express self-control in my talk. It requires great and constant effort.

> *"All kinds of animals, birds, reptiles and creatures of the sea are being tamed and have been tamed by man, but no man can tame the tongue. It is a restless evil, full of deadly poison" (James 3:7–8).*

Think about taming a horse. You can actually get this powerful animal to let you stuff a metal bit in its mouth, cinch a leather strap around its flank, and climb on its back for a ride. Pretty impressive. To say nothing about training Rover to roll over or Flipper to jump through hoops or Dumbo to dance.

Wild, willful animals can be trained. It just takes great patience and effort. But even with perseverance and hard work, it is an uphill challenge to train the mouth.

Hope from the source.

Now, all these words of ours do not form in a vacuum. They come from somewhere. They have a source. Jesus said that our words are an overflow from our heart. It is as if our soul is a warehouse, with good or evil stock-piled. When we speak, we're just drawing on our inventory. Words, he said, are such a reliable indicator of what is inside us, that it would be fair to judge us by our words (Matthew 12:34–37). "By your words you will be acquitted, and by your words you will be condemned," he said.

James expresses the same idea, then illustrates it. "Can both fresh water and salt water flow from the same spring? Do fig trees produce olives?" Of course not. The tree is consistent, and so is the spring (James 3:9–12)—they can only produce what is in them.

But I am more complicated. I open my mouth, and either good or evil flows, depending, I suppose, on which source I'm tapping into. To put it another way, if we want to know what controls us, all we need to do is listen.

That morning on the bus I added my voice to "Nerd Neck's" ridicule with scarcely a thought. I began to deal with the consequences soon after in the parking lot. I still have a scar on my lip from that fight. But I have often wondered what scars were left on the other guy by all the insensitive and unkind words of that bus ride.

Because of that morning, I no longer question the power of words.

But I often ask myself: how am I using the power?

Monday Checkpoint: *Words*

Ever say something in an unguarded moment and then feel like a fool?

☞ Think about it . . .

I would hate to think I was the only one; for as careful as I try to be with my words, I know I have muttered some pretty stupid stuff. I've heard words come out of my mouth and wondered where they came from. I've tossed some verbal darts and watched as they found their mark and caused their pain.

And I've heard some painful words. I have been on the receiving end of angry words, hateful words, taunting words. I have felt their sting.

Think for a moment of the words that have hurt you or the words you have used to hurt others. It doesn't take much. A small spark can set off a raging inferno. We regret the words, but the damage goes on, long after the sound has faded. It's one of the mysteries of speech: once spoken, words hang around to haunt us.

But let's turn the idea around for a minute. If something so small as an unkind word can do such damage, how much good could come from a kind word, an encouraging word, a wise word?

☞ God's Word says . . .

"Consider what a great forest is set on fire by a small spark" (James 3:5).

☞ Make it a prayer . . .

Lord, as your words have changed me, may my words change others—for good.

Tuesday Checkpoint: *Words*

If we want to know what we're like, all we have to do is listen to ourselves.

☞ Think about it . . .

I once ended a fight with four one-syllable words. "You're just like Dad!"

My father was an honest man, a fair man, a hard-working man. But when I looked into my brother's face and spat out those four words—"You're just like Dad!"—I was not thinking of my father's virtues. I was not complimenting my big brother. I was in the middle of an argument that had become increasingly physical—a fight I could not hope to win.

As the battle got out of hand, I resorted to the verbal equivalent of nuclear arms. I scanned my mind for words that would wound. And I found them. My brother struggled with a fiery temper, much as my father did. After an outburst of rage, regret came. Sharing my father's anger was my brother's fear. I knew that, and I used it against him.

"You're just like Dad!" Immediately, the room was quiet, the shouting stilled. The look on my brother's face told me all I needed to know. Those words had found their mark. But those words also measured me, and they showed me how small I had become.

☞ God's Word says . . .

"We all stumble in many ways. If anyone is never at fault in what he says, he is a perfect man, able to keep his whole body in check" (James 3:2).

☞ Make it a prayer . . .

Father, tame my words!

Wednesday Checkpoint: *Words*

How powerful are words? Remember the times they've helped. Remember the times they've hurt.

Think about it . . .

Words are windows. You can "look" through them, and see what's in a person's soul. That's why words are so powerful—they express what is held most deeply within the person who speaks, and they touch what is held most deeply in the person who hears. Oh sure, we say things we don't mean. Words that should not be taken seriously. Words that if we thought about them we don't even believe. But even those careless, inaccurate words show our soul.

Words are windows. You can "look" through them and see the fires of hell. The Bible says our evil words are ignited by hellish flames. Criticism, ridicule, gossip. Damaging words give a glimpse of torment.

Words are windows. You can "look" through them and see the landscape of heaven. Words don't have to hurt. When we speak an encouraging word—a word of praise or kindness—we are drawing aside a curtain on all that is good. Our words have just such power.

God's Word says . . .

"The tongue is a fire, a world of evil among the parts of the body. It corrupts the whole person, sets the whole course of his life on fire, and is itself set on fire by hell" (James 3:6).

Make it a prayer . . .

Touch me. Change me. Let my words be a window on a transformed soul.

✓ Thursday Checkpoint: *Words*

Why is it so hard to tame the tongue? What makes it so complicated to control our words?

☞ Think about it . . .

Mouths are easy enough to operate. Hinged at the jaw, they move up and down. We've learned how to form words, express ideas, speak our mind. The frustration comes because it's like we've learned to start a car, put it in gear, and give it the gas, but we've never figured out how to stop it. How do we decrease speed? Where's the brake? How do we switch this motor off? Our mouths get started and we can't shut them up. One word, and we're well on the road to regret.

It could seem a bleak picture. The Bible says, "No man can tame the tongue." Animals, birds, reptiles, creatures of the sea—these we can tame. It seems silly to think our own mouth could have its way, against our will. "No man can tame the tongue." Training our talk is outside the realm of human achievement.

It is, however, something that God can do. He can change our talk. He can transform our words.

☞ God's Word says . . .

"All kinds of animals, birds, reptiles and creatures of the sea are being tamed and have been tamed by man, but no man can tame the tongue. It is a restless evil, full of deadly poison" (James 3:7–8).

☞ Make it a prayer . . .

Encourage me, Lord. Tame my talk. Show me signs of progress on this that I cannot do alone.

Friday Checkpoint: Words

If you could open the door of your soul, you'd find a warehouse. Now, what do you have hidden in all those containers?

☞ Think about it . . .

Jesus said that our words are an overflow of our heart. Bad words flow out of the bad stuff within us; good words are drawn from deep down inside goodness. The soul *is* a warehouse, with both good and evil stockpiled. When we speak, we are merely drawing on our inventory.

In saying this, Jesus has given us a clue to how we can change our talk. For my words to be different, my heart must first change. If I put better stuff in my warehouse, the shipments will improve. I will deliver the goods. My words will have greater value and benefit.

James uses the illustration of a spring. If good water is flowing, it's because there is good at its source. When true faith enters my life, it sets a process in motion. It begins purifying the spring right there at the source—the soul. As I fill my mind with Scripture, that purifying process accelerates. Before I know it, I am tasting good words, instead of bitter regret.

☞ God's Word says . . .

"Out of the same mouth come praise and cursing. My brothers, this should not be. Can both fresh water and salt water flow from the same spring?" (James 3:10–11).

☞ Make It a prayer . . .

Let the words of my mouth and the meditations of my heart be acceptable to you, Lord, my strength and my redeemer.

Week 8

Wisdom

James 3:13–17

First Impressions

Most unexpectedly, I found the difference between foolishness and wisdom.

Things are not always what they first appear to be. Bob, for instance.

I don't remember when I first met him because I hardly noticed him initially. Maybe he transferred into our school. Maybe he had been there all along. It was as if I had never really seen him, probably because he was so ordinary. It did not occur to me that we might become friends. Then one afternoon we wound up at the same table in the cafeteria. Our conversation turned toward music, and we found a common area of interest that eventually led us to friendship.

Things are not always what they at first appear to be.

My friendship with Bob is one example, music itself is another. I can think of musicians whose sound was so different that when I first heard them, I wrote them off as weird. Their music was unappealing. But after I listened more carefully, I heard them in a new way. My opinion shifted.

Think of a movie that starts slow. An odd story line makes it hard to get into. But twenty minutes later, the pace picks up; you get some idea where the film is going.

That describes perfectly how faith came to me.

How my view changed. How I discovered the difference between foolishness and wisdom.

I knew a few religious people. Some seemed odd. Their lives emptied of anything fun. One or two even seemed mean. Unpleasant to be around. Others seemed so *good* I could never measure up. To be Christian would mean endless guilt and frustration.

As a result, my first impression was: to be Christian would mean *loss*, giving something up. Life would be less. It would be boring.

That first impression kept me away from Christianity for a long time. I was afraid of it. All those Bible words seemed wise and good, but I was certain it would cost too much if I were to take it all seriously. So I distanced myself from faith. I stayed just close enough to feel a little religious, but not close enough to truly know God. I listened to the wise religious ideas, but I had no idea how to act on them—and little desire to do so.

I later discovered that, like so many things, Christianity was not what it at first appeared to be.

Two things changed my mind.

First, I met people who claimed to be Christian yet were refreshingly normal. Where had they been? Why hadn't I noticed them before? They were fun to be with. They were reasonably intelligent. They were disarmingly kind. They seemed to have been deeply changed by all this religious wisdom. I began telling myself, *Maybe my first impression about Christianity was wrong.*

The other thing that began to change the way I thought about faith was the Bible itself. I started reading it more open-mindedly, and what I read amazed me.

I had thought of Christianity as an interruption to life. An unpleasantness tacked on. Sort of a Sunday intrusion that disrupted life every week. I had thought of all the negatives: rules and regulations programmed into Christian brain cells, making it impossible "to get any rest" or have any fun. If I became a Christian, I reasoned, the old conscience would scream instead of whisper, giving me perpetual spiritual headaches.

But now as I read the Bible, faith appeared more than an add-on or an interruption or an intrusion disrupting life. For true Christians, it seemed, Christianity *was* life. The religious wisdom became a part of them. It changed the way they saw *everything.* And because their view changed, true Christians did not resent the faith that changed them. They did not fight against it. They welcomed it.

Another way to look at laws.

In time, I concluded that true Christians didn't force themselves to do good in order to silence a screaming conscience, they did good because faith had begun to make them good. That is, because of their faith, they now *wanted* to be different. If you *want* it, you don't consider it so unpleasant. The good change that followed their new desires became a proof that they had found true faith and wisdom.

> *"Who is wise and understanding among you? Let him show it by his good life, by deeds done in the humility that comes from wisdom"* (James 3:13).

What I *think* and *how I act* are fused together and cannot be separated. I am wise if I live right; living right proves I am wise.

This was not my first impression of Christianity. But how could I argue against it? I had met people who lived like this—people who were glad to have found a faith that was changing everything about them.

The flip side of faith.

Not everyone who claimed to be Christian was so pleasant to be around, of course. As I mentioned above, some were odd or mean. Hypocrites and grumps were easy to find. But did religious fakes disprove faith? Just because there were fools in the church, did that mean there was no one truly wise?

I found that the Bible even talked honestly about this.

> *"If you harbor bitter envy and selfish ambition in your hearts, do not boast about it or deny the truth. Such 'wisdom' does not come down from heaven but is earthly, unspiritual, of the devil. For where you have envy and selfish ambition, there you find disorder and every evil practice"* (James 3:14–16).

That pretty well described some "Christians" I had known. Perhaps they just had the wise religious ideas on the *outside* but never quite made those ideas a part of who they were on the inside.

Coming out of hiding.

One day I realized that I had been keeping Jesus at arm's length. And I knew why. I had been hiding behind the hypocrites and behind my wrong ideas—my false first impressions of faith.

I started thinking about the best people I knew—the people I wanted to be like. Most of them had one thing in common: Jesus. He was important to them. And he was changing the way they thought and lived.

They were becoming wise, and that wisdom was making them better. They were good. They were thoughtful. They were fair. And I realized: if what they said was true, I could be like them. I could be like Jesus.

> *"The wisdom that comes from heaven is first of all pure; then peace-loving, considerate, submissive, full of mercy and good fruit, impartial and sincere" (James 3:17).*

Things are not always what they at first appear to be. Sometimes they are far better. An unexpected friendship. Extraordinary music. An intriguing movie. Even a "religious experience."

I now know what I wish I had known sooner: you can have a life-changing wisdom on the inside—as part of who you are.

My first impression was wrong. Christianity does not mean loss. It means life.

Monday Checkpoint: *Wisdom*

Things aren't always what they seem to be.

Think about it . . .

We could take a little test. I start a sentence, you complete it. Here we go:

"When I think of the church, I . . ."

"Faith is . . ."

"Christians are . . ."

There was a time when I would have completed those phrases something like this: "When I think of the church, I . . . *gag.*" "Faith is . . . *boring.*" "Christians are . . . *impossible.*"

Over the years, my views shifted. "When I think of the church, I . . . *think of people trying to encourage one another.*" "Faith is . . . *life.*" "Christians are . . . *God's kids, learning to be like Jesus.*"

At some point, I started focusing less on people and more on Christ. We pattern our life after *him.* When I took a closer look at Jesus, my view of the church began to change. Faith took on a new meaning. I thought of Christians differently. But this new way of seeing began with a new look at Christ. Jesus was not boring, unpleasant, or unkind. It's God's aim to make us like Christ. If we wind up sour and boring and mean, something's wrong. Faith is all about Jesus. And that is very, very cool.

God's Word says . . .

Jesus said, "I have come that they may have life, and have it to the full" (John 10:10).

Make it a prayer . . .

Lord, show me this life Jesus came to give me.

Tuesday Checkpoint: *Wisdom*

I met people who claimed to be Christian yet were refreshingly normal. Why hadn't I noticed them before?

Think about it ...

The problem with spectator sports is you *can* go to the game and ignore the action. Other things can distract you. You may pay more attention to what's happening on the sidelines or at the concession stands. If you choose to, you can spend the whole game disengaged.

For me, faith was a spectator sport. I went to church—I'm not sure why—and I watched people play religion. Things changed only when I began to see faith as a *participation* sport, something that involved *me* and all of my life. Everything looked different once I got into the game, instead of watching Sunday go by from the sidelines.

Once faith had my attention—and my participation—I started noticing other people who were truly in the game. Christians who were refreshingly normal yet consumed by their faith. Jesus had moved to the center of their lives—the center of *my* life—how could anything remain the same?

God's Word says ...

"To live is Christ" (Philippians 1:21).

Make it a prayer ...

Lord, keep me involved in the game of faith, living life with Jesus in the center. And keep me "refreshingly normal," not stuffy and boring.

Wednesday Checkpoint: *Wisdom*

If you try to force yourself to be good, you'll probably fail. Want to find a better way?

☞ Think about it . . .

You're standing under a hot sky and the air is heavy with humidity. Perspiration streams down your face and chest. Before you is an acre of tall grass, sloping up toward the house. Your hands are on this new mower, idling noisily in front of you. There's a job to be done, and you lean into it. After pushing the heavy machine through four or five swatches, your arms aching, your brother strides up to you, laughing and pointing. His lips are moving, but you can't hear him over the roar of the five-horse engine. You hit the kill-switch, and he tells you, still laughing, "You know, jerk, this mower *is* self-propelled. You don't have to push it like that."

It's true, of course. Once the drive mechanism is engaged, the machine does the work. Your effort is required too, but not to keep the machine moving.

You *can* do good through your own effort—up to a point. But it is exhausting work. What true faith does is to put a new drive inside you. You do good because you want to. Your desires have changed.

☞ God's Word says . . .

"Who is wise and understanding among you? Let him show it by his good life, by deeds done in the humility that comes from wisdom" (James 3:13).

☞ Make it a prayer . . .

Thank you that you are alive in me, motivating me to do good.

Thursday Checkpoint: *Wisdom*

Hypocrites, grumps, and meanies—they're not hard to find, even in the church. But now, what's the point?

☞ Think about it ...

I used to go to a church where people fought a lot—somewhat openly. My friends and I sometimes went to business meetings simply because we knew there'd be fireworks. Certain people could be counted on to raise a ruckus, and we thought that was pretty funny. Later, looking back, it just seemed sad.

The church's reputation for cantankerousness kept some people away and kept others focused on the wrong thing.

God is doing remarkable things in the world. He is not doing them through hypocrites, grumps, and meanies. He is not doing his work through bitterness and envy and self-centeredness.

I don't want to be a distraction to what God is doing. I don't want to be out of step with Jesus. So I take my eyes off of the hypocrites and I ignore the grumps.

Now, with our eyes on Jesus, let's change the world!

☞ God's Word says ...

"If you harbor bitter envy and selfish ambition in your hearts, do not boast about it or deny the truth. Such 'wisdom' does not come down from heaven, but is earthly, unspiritual, of the devil" (James 3:14–15).

☞ Make it a prayer ...

Father, keep me free of envy, pride, and selfishness. Keep my eyes on Jesus, and Jesus only.

Friday Checkpoint: *Wisdom*

It was a shocking discovery. Most of the people I wanted to be like had one thing in common: Jesus.

☞ Think about it . . .

I did not particularly want to be thought of as a Bible-banger. If halos glowed and showed, I'd just as soon have checked mine at the door. A reputation for religion? I'll pass. Maybe it was this reticence, this fear of being "too good," that kept me from paying attention at church. Maybe I squinted my eyes shut against true faith because I was afraid all that light streaming through stained glass might somehow zap me with holiness. I was sure God's math skills were limited—he could only subtract; he could not add. He could take things away from me, but it never occurred to me that he could *add* to my life.

For a time, I rather liked the reputation of being a rebel. Not scummy, necessarily, just a bit on the edge. Not an out-and-out delinquent, but flirting with trouble.

Gradually, I realized: I did not really want to be *bad*. The people I admired were kind, forgiving, generous people. They were, I realized with a shock, *good* people. Goodness was what I wanted after all, and I found it in Jesus.

☞ God's Word says . . .

"The wisdom that comes from heaven is first of all pure; then peace-loving, considerate, submissive, full of mercy and good fruit, impartial and sincere" (James 3:17).

☞ Make it a prayer . . .

Lord, my first impression was wrong. Faith does not mean loss. It means life.

Week 9

Devotion

James 4:1–10

Weekend Reading

Sleeping with the Enemy

> As long as I am guided by a deep love for God—and a true caring for people—I will not destroy myself.

Eric returned home from a late band practice to find his parents fighting again. As he stepped into the house, he felt that now-familiar tightening in his chest. His head throbbed. His stomach muscles cramped. As his parents' problems had intensified over the past months, Eric had felt their stress. It had become his.

Lately, the fighting was almost constant. Mom had hinted of Dad having an affair with one of her friends, a suggestion of betrayal that Eric had tried to ignore.

Eric walked from the back door through the kitchen. His dad sat at the table, filtering through the day's mail. His mom stood near him, confronting him about something. He would not look up and was not returning her verbal fire.

"You've been seeing her, sleeping with her!" She spat the words, tears streaking down her face.

Eric had passed quickly through the room; he had no interest in sharing directly in their conflict. But when he heard his mother's accusation so flatly stated, Eric stopped and turned, caught by emotions he could not explain. “Mom,” Eric said, hopefulness coloring his voice, “don’t jump to conclusions!”

His mother, who had not acknowledged Eric’s presence until that moment, glanced at her son, then down at her silent husband. “Did you hear what he said! ‘Don’t jump to conclusions!’” As she repeated her son’s words, they too became an accusation.

Still, Eric’s dad stared downward. He did not so much as murmur a denial. Neither did he express remorse. He simply went on shuffling the day’s mail. Eric knew, beyond question, it was true. It was all true. His dad had been unfaithful.

Eric felt intense emotion. His dad was spreading his unfaithfulness to the whole family. Eric’s mom was not the only one betrayed; Eric was betrayed as well.

Suppose it was your father or your mother who’d been sleeping around. Can you feel the emotion? A knot twisting in your stomach. A dull ache pounding in your skull. A heaviness pressing against your chest.

Then put yourself in the position of the betrayer. Suppose you were the unfaithful father. How would you feel, knowing your own dark side had consumed your life? You have hurt the people who ought to mean the most to you. You have catered to yourself and brought pain to those who trusted you.

Eric’s experience—and that of his family—captures the emotion of betrayal. The feeling unfaithfulness brings. And this is the feeling I create in God when I turn from his ways. He calls it adultery and tells me he feels a deep, piercing jealousy. He aches to have me return, truly sorry, eager (with his help) to change.

Eric's experience is real. It happened. But this is just as real: I have hurt God in the same way Eric's father hurt him.

I must discover how to end the pain.

Wanting the wrong thing in life ruins life itself.

Eric's father probably felt some sense of emptiness and tried to fill it in the wrong way. In the process, he ruined life for himself and for those around him.

> *"What causes fights and quarrels among you? Don't they come from desires that battle within you?" (James 4:1).*

Of course, the wrong desires are not always sexual. Sometimes it is the drive to be accepted, and it leads us into dishonesty or compromise. Jealousy takes hold of my life. Or bitterness. There is a way out of these negative feelings, but will I take it? Or will I let my wrong desires—whatever they may be—eat away at my life and my relationships until there is nothing of value left?

Desire is an unusual sensation. Wrong desires so easily become destructive obsessions. I work at *getting*, regardless of the cost to my character. Take greed, jealousy, pornography, or substance abuse as examples.

Good desires, on the other hand, build me up. When I crave what is right, I become a better person.

> *"You want something but don't get it. You kill and covet.... You do not have because you do not ask God. When you ask, you do not receive, because you ask*

with wrong motives, that you may spend what you get on your pleasure" (James 4:2–3).

I may read these words and say, "I never wanted anything so badly that I would kill for it." But that's not quite the point.

There are two ways to get something: fighting and asking. When we want what's wrong, when we go after what we should not have, it is often a fight—a struggle to obtain it.

When we want the right thing, for the right reasons, we may simply ask and receive. Here is one example: "Those who hunger and thirst for righteousness . . . will be filled" (Matthew 5:6).

Wrong ruins life; right fulfills it.

There is no neutral territory.

I am tossing around the words "right" and "wrong" as if there is no middle ground between them, as if everything in life is either good or bad. Isn't anything neutral?

The Bible is filled with commands. Things I should do. Things I must never do. But the lists are hardly comprehensive. Consider your average week. Is there a list of laws so long that it covers everything? Of course not. So much is "neutral."

Or is it?

Jesus once spoke to people who were trying to fabricate the perfect list, a code of law so comprehensive that it would cover everything. What did he tell them? "Don't worry so much about the list, just love God—and people. If you do, you will keep the law automatically."

As long as I am guided by a deep love for God—and a true care for people—I will not destroy myself and others with wrong desires. I will not bring pain into my relationship with God. But this love must motivate all I do. When it does, it will turn even the neutral things into good.

When I forget this love relationship and turn toward selfish motives—greed, lust, jealousy—I am betraying God. I am sleeping with the enemy.

> *"You adulterous people, don't you know that friendship with the world is hatred toward God? Anyone who chooses to be a friend of the world becomes an enemy of God. Or do you think Scripture says without reason that the spirit he caused to live in us envies intensely?" (James 4:4–5).*

God wants us!

It hurts him when we turn away.

These words—adultery, hatred, enmity, and envy—bring me back to Eric and his family. What did Eric want to see in his father there in the kitchen? Deep inside, Eric seemed to sense his mother's accusations were true. He probably did not want his father simply to deny the charges out of defensiveness. But what might have happened had his father looked up, broken and full of remorse? What might have happened had he embraced his family, asked forgiveness, sought counseling, changed his ways?

Sure, there would have been anger, hurt, distrust. Unfaithfulness carries devastating consequences. Even so, there could have been healing. Eric could have forgiven; his mom could have accepted sincere apology and worked for a new beginning.

God does that with us.

Over and over again.

It requires action and initiative to stay where I want to be: with God.

But when I simply turn toward God, he *runs* toward me.

> *"'God opposes the proud, but gives grace to the humble.' Submit yourselves, then, to God. Resist the devil, and he will flee from you. Come near to God and he will come near to you. Wash your hands, you sinners, and purify your hearts, you double-minded. Grieve, mourn and wail. Change your laughter to mourning and your joy to gloom. Humble yourselves before the Lord, and he will lift you up" (James 4:6–10).*

Grieve, mourn, wail, gloom are strong words that sound like death. But isn't that what living in unfaithfulness truly is? When Eric's father betrayed the family, didn't something die? Something inside Eric. Something inside his mother. Would apology have seemed sincere had Eric's dad only lightheartedly acknowledged the affair? Something in the family had *died*. Grief would be appropriate, but grief does not last forever.

Isn't it truly remarkable that even in the worst of our sins, even when we have been sleeping with the enemy, God is willing to welcome us home?

What are we waiting for?

Monday Checkpoint: *Devotion*

It sounds strange to say it: God is jealous.

Think about it . . .

I remember the first time I heard it: "God is a jealous God." My immediate thought was, "Well, then God has a problem. Jealousy is wrong, isn't it?"

The problem is, when you're talking about something as difficult to comprehend as *God*, words are so inadequate. So the Bible uses "art." It paints pictures with words—it creates a portrait—to help us "see" what God is like.

When God's people got bored with him, when they lost interest in him and started looking into other religions, the Bible said those people were committing adultery. They were "married" to God but sleeping with someone else. That's how it felt to God. Their "unfaithfulness" hurt him. God felt like we feel when we're jealous. He felt betrayed and cheated. And he felt that way because of *love*. If he didn't love us, it wouldn't matter. Our disinterest would cause him no pain.

Our devotion is not something God can take or leave. He is not passive toward us. He loves us. We matter to him. Our fidelity is something he treasures. He expects an exclusive, faithful relationship.

God's Word says . . .

God says, "I have loved you with an everlasting love" (Jeremiah 31:3).

Make it a prayer . . .

I love you, Lord. If I ever allow anything to come between us, please show me what it is, and call me back to an exclusive, faithful relationship with you.

Tuesday Checkpoint: *Devotion*

We are free to desire anything. But what if we want the wrong things? What happens then?

☞ Think about it . . .

What happens? When we want the wrong things, we may end up destroying everything that truly matters. Wrong desires quickly become obsessions. Our drive to be accepted by others leads us to compromise. Envy, bitterness, greed, pornography, substance abuse. Give wrong desires one square inch, and they quickly take over all the real estate.

There is a battle raging. Wrong desires are at war within us. If our loyalties lean away from true faith and toward those wrong desires, soon enough we will be filled with regret. We may get what we think we want and lose everything of true value.

Take an inventory of your affection. What matters to you? You can get a fairly accurate idea by asking yourself a few questions. Consider your daydreams. What fills your mind? How do you use your time? How do you spend your money? What excites you most? What can you hardly wait to discuss with your friends? What bores you, and what gets your full and undivided attention?

☞ God's Word says . . .

"What causes fights and quarrels among you? Don't they come from desires that battle within you?" (James 4:1).

☞ Make it a prayer . . .

Lord, I admit it. There is a war of conflicting desires within me. Turn my heart toward you.

Wednesday Checkpoint: *Devotion*

The difference between right and wrong can be summed up in two very different words: "fighting" and "asking."

☞ Think about it . . .

When I want the wrong thing, I wind up fighting to get it. I *feel* the war inside.

When I want the right thing, it is enough to ask.

What do you most want in life? Popularity? There's nothing wrong with wanting friends. But if popularity becomes too important, you may wind up making compromises to get it.

Money makes life easier—in some ways, at least. In other ways, it complicates it. How badly do you want money? Jesus said you cannot love God and money, because if you love money, it will distract your attention, taking your focus off the things that are most important. Check out what Jesus had to say on the subject (Matthew 6:19–24).

We can ask for anything, but when desire becomes obsession, beware!

There are other things, important things, that are ours for the asking—ours for the *desiring*. Jesus said, "Those who hunger and thirst for righteousness will be filled" (Matthew 5:6). "Seek first his kingdom and his righteousness" and God will meet every legitimate need we face (Matthew 6:33).

☞ God's Word says . . .

"You do not have, because you do not ask God. When you ask, you do not receive, because you ask with wrong motives" (James 4:2–3).

☞ Make it a prayer . . .

Father, give me good desires—desires you are pleased to meet.

Thursday Checkpoint: *Devotion*

It is a dangerous mistake to think that somewhere in life there is a "demilitarized zone." There is no neutral ground.

Think about it . . .

In truth, good and evil fight over every square inch of our lives. This can be confusing. We might wish that everything was clear-cut, black-and-white. Can you imagine your life *labeled*? Everything tagged "good" or "evil"? Every possession, every activity, every individual?

Instead of an *Encyclopedia Britannica* of good and evil, God has given us a few laws and some clear principles. You can sum it up like this: "Love God, and love people." When in doubt, let that simple idea guide you.

Should I do this, go there, buy that, read this, see that, spend my time listening to this or doing the other thing? Well, does it help you love God more? Is it an expression of your love for people? Or does it draw your mind away from God and make you less sensitive to those around you?

You cannot cover every inch of life with black or white labels. You cannot sort every little thing into piles of good and stacks of evil. But loitering around every decision, each activity, all our moments, is the potential to forget God and wander off, or to love him even more deeply and follow him more closely.

God's Word says . . .

"Anyone who chooses to be a friend of the world becomes an enemy of God" (James 4:4).

Make it a prayer . . .

Lord, you have my heart. All of it.

Friday Checkpoint: *Devotion*

If you simply turn toward God, he will run to you.

☞ Think about it . . .

Can you see God hitching up those long, flowing robes we imagine him to be wearing, and then sprinting toward us? Can you see him running up to you, then stopping, his breath coming in deep gasps, like a sprinter who's just crossed the finish line and broken the tape? Can you *feel* arms encircling you, welcoming you home, when all you've done is to change your mind and turn toward him?

One afternoon, Jesus' closest friends asked him about forgiveness. "Lord, how many times shall I forgive my brother when he sins against me? Up to seven times?" Peter was asking the question, and I suppose the number seemed outrageously high to him. A surprise was coming. Jesus answered, "I tell you, not seven times, but seventy-seven times." Or perhaps even "seventy times seven."

I like the story, because it suggests to me that if *people* are expected to forgive and forgive and forgive, how much more will God forgive me and forgive me and forgive me? I have failed him. I have betrayed him. I have been unfaithful to him. In all likelihood, it will happen again. But every time I turn back toward God, he drops everything and comes running.

☞ God's Word says . . .

"Resist the devil, and he will flee from you. Come near to God and he will come near to you" (James 4:7–8).

☞ Make it a prayer . . .

Thank you. Again.

Week 10

Judgment

James 4:11–12

Weekend Reading

The Problem with Judgment

When I criticize you, I hurt us both.

We used to laugh at Chester, the bald-headed church custodian. He dressed oddly, and his manners were peculiar (the word that comes to mind is "hick"), though he was friendly.

Chester had a funny way of saying "Hello!" I cannot capture it in writing. You just had the feeling he ought to be in bib overalls and holding a pitchfork whenever he talked.

We mocked him.

We made up stories about him.

Our church held classes in a huge old house, which, on rainy nights, could easily have passed for a haunted mansion. One afternoon, while rummaging around in the attic, we found the cover from a ceiling light fixture, a round glass globe. After noting the resemblance to Chester's hairless head, we ceremoniously placed it in the center of the attic floor, then we added a little sign: CHESTER RUNS THE CHURCH. HE CONTROLS IT FROM HERE.

Okay, just a stupid joke.

Later, though, I wondered if Chester discovered it. Certainly it would hurt his feelings had he known how much we laughed at him, if he had any idea how many silly stories we fabricated at his expense, if he noticed how we mimicked his "backward accent."

We had a volunteer youth leader who freely gave his time to do things with us. He even gave up vacation days to take us on outings. But we didn't like him. He had a dumb haircut and narrow ideas. He would not let us dance at youth group parties, even though (and I quote): "I met my wife at a dance." One Sunday night at a youth meeting, all evening, we argued with him about dancing.

After that, things got out of hand. We talked about him behind his back. We got one another worked up, sharing our complaints and negative opinions until we very nearly hated him.

His name was Louie. We started calling him "Screwy Louie." Finally, he quit.

Now I realize he must have been extremely discouraged—he'd given us so much but got only grief in return.

Not long after Louie quit as youth sponsor, Mary, a high-school girl, started coming to our church. Mary was friendly enough but had a reputation for loose morals. Guys said she'd sleep with anyone. The girls looked on her as if she were dirt.

We all sent out clear messages to Mary, letting her know that she was not welcome at our church. No one would sit with her. People even got up and moved when she took the risk of sitting near them. We ignored her too. We did not make room for her in our conversations. It wasn't long before we got just what we wanted: sinful Mary left the church. For good.

Even then I knew the truth. Most of us were no better off than she. Most of the guys would have gladly had sex with her had they only had the opportunity. One of the girls who had been so judgmental of Mary was herself pregnant not long after wicked Mary had been chased away.

One way or another, all us hypocrites had sins we tried to hide. Were we really any better than Mary? All she wanted, it seemed, was friendship. But we turned her away from the church—and away from God!

It is frightening to have that on your conscience.

And then there was Eric, whose dad betrayed the family with his unfaithfulness. Eric would complain to us about his dad. He told us his dad was having an affair. He told us how his dad would fight with his mom and how he'd yell at the family. The family was crumbling, all because of Eric's stupid father.

Was there ever a problem so obviously one-sided as the problem with Eric's dad? The family, it seemed, had done nothing to hurt this man, yet he betrayed them all.

Eric's anger turned to bitterness, and we, his friends, fueled that fire. We told him how awful his dad was, never stopping to think how our comments made it so much harder for Eric ever to forgive his father.

We would not so much have suggested that Eric *should* forgive his father. The idea would have seemed preposterous to us.

There are things you notice only later, when you have the time and perspective to look back.

Now I know that I hurt an old church custodian with my mocking laughter. Now I see how hateful I was to an unselfish youth group sponsor who was only interested in my welfare. Now I realize that sinful, friendless Mary may have formed a negative opinion of God based on the cruelty of some of his followers. Now I understand how my hasty agreement with Eric—"Yes, your dad's an idiot!"—made it harder for him to see the problem objectively, to love his father, and to forgive him.

Each of these stories reminds me why it is so wrong to judge people or slander them. And I read these Bible words, knowing they were written for me:

> *"Do not slander one another. Anyone who speaks against his brother or judges him speaks against the law and judges it. When you judge the law, you are not keeping it, but sitting in judgment on it. There is only one Lawgiver and Judge, the one who is able to save and destroy. But you—who are you to judge your neighbor?" (James 4:11–12).*

An odd idea, hard to decipher:

If I speak against you, I speak against God's Law.

If I judge you, I judge God's Law.

What's the point?

It is not my job to judge you. It is not my place to speak against you.

Mocking Chester, fighting Screwy Louie, judging Eric's father—who did we think we were?

It is the job of the Law and God, the Lawgiver, to point out wrong and show the way to what is right. I may help in the process, but it must be with humility and love, not slander and judgment.

> *"If someone is caught in a sin, you who are spiritual should restore him gently. But watch yourself, or you also may be tempted" (Galatians 6:1).*

That certainly was not my approach. The idea of "restoring" or helping these people never entered my mind. I just wanted to mock them or judge them.

When I take over and step into God's job as Judge and Lawgiver, I insult him. It is as if I am saying: "Your law is not clear enough. You are not doing your job. You need *my* help!"

And he says:

> *"There is only one Lawgiver and Judge, the one who is able to save and destroy. But you—who are you to judge your neighbor?" (James 4:12).*

Who am *I*?

Chester needed respect. Louie needed appreciation. Mary needed friendship. Eric needed quiet support.

Some of them needed restoration. None of them needed my judgment.

In my criticism, I failed.

Monday Checkpoint: *Judgment*

Chester was hurt. Louie was discouraged. Mary was lonely. Eric was confused. And I didn't care.

Think about it . . .

When it's working as it ought to work, the church is amazing. When Christians are acting as God intends them to act, people are astounded. There are few places in the world as safe, as wonderful, as encouraging as a good church. Christian friends love one another, forgive one another, help one another, call for the best in one another.

What could be better?

We need acceptance. We find it at church. We need people who will be honest with us, who will help keep us in line. Christian friends lovingly do just that. We cannot survive for long without encouragement. You will find it in God's family.

Churches aren't perfect. They rarely measure up to what we need them to be. But even with their imperfections, circles of Christian friendship are astoundingly helpful.

People will come to your church hurt, discouraged, lonely, confused. Sometimes Christians will make these problems worse. But here's some good news. One caring person can help lift the hurt, dispel the discouragement, ease the loneliness, sort out the confusion. One caring person can make up for the failures of many others who remain indifferent. And that one caring person could be you.

God's Word says . . .

"Let us consider how we may spur one another on toward love and good deeds" (Hebrews 10:24).

Make it a prayer . . .

Lord, make me a person who is known for encouragement.

Tuesday Checkpoint: *Judgment*

The idea is to minimize your regrets.

Think about it . . .

In the next few moments, we could focus on the sting of regret. We could think back over today, yesterday, life up to this point. We could replay scenes of our own hatefulness. We could relive our failures. We could say, "If I had it to do over again . . . ," and complete that phrase with a hundred different conclusions—things we would do differently, if only we could.

We could focus on our regrets, and there would be some value to that. But couldn't we also remember those times when a kind word from us lifted the spirits of a discouraged friend? Couldn't we think of the times we saw a smile spread across a parent's face because of some unexpected word of appreciation from us? Aren't there times we can recall when we stood up and said the right thing and changed the outcome of a decision?

A moment's thought, and we remember what we hope never to do again. A moment's thought, and we recall what we hope to repeat over and over.

God's Word says . . .

"Do not slander one another. Anyone who speaks against his brother or judges him speaks against the law and judges it. When you judge the law, you are not keeping it, but sitting in judgment on it" (James 4:11).

Make it a prayer . . .

Thank you, Lord, that even my failures are not wasted, if they change the way I live today.

Wednesday Checkpoint: *Judgment*

Who would be so silly as to sub for God? To fill in for the divine? To presume to take God's place?

☞ Think about it . . .

Guess what? Every time we judge others, that's precisely what we're doing—horning in on God's territory, pushing him aside so we can take over his job.

Unfortunately, we do not have the qualifications to be the Lawgiver or the Judge. We are not wise enough. We lack knowledge. We cannot look deeply enough into the motives of those we judge. We lack understanding of their hardships, their background, their experience.

We are not kind enough to be the Judge. We are short on mercy. We barely comprehend grace. We do not know what it means to love someone unconditionally. We lack experience in the art of forgiveness. We are not practiced at looking into someone's eyes and seeing their sincere desire to change.

We are not good enough to be the Judge. We lack holiness. We do not perfectly live the law ourselves. These lives of ours fall short of being the good examples we would hope for in a judge. The Judge should mirror the goodness of the Law. We should see its virtue, reflected in his life.

☞ God's Word says . . .

"There is only one Lawgiver and Judge, the one who is able to save and destroy. But you—who are you to judge your neighbor?" (James 4:12).

☞ Make it a prayer . . .

Thank you, perfect Father, that you and you alone are the Lawgiver and the Judge.

Thursday Checkpoint: *Judgment*

A friend is tangled up in wrong. What can we do to help?

Think about it . . .

There are different ways to help.

(1) We can *warn*. Sometimes the greatest display of kindness is a gentle word of caution. We see the direction someone is headed. We know that course will bring heartache. We can foresee the regret that will inevitably come. In kindness, we offer a word of warning.

(2) We can *encourage*. We can point the way to better decisions. We can call to mind the good result that will most certainly flow from wise choices. We can be a friend to lean on; we can offer a shoulder to cry on. We can be there, reminding that friend that she is not the first one—not the *only* one—to fall. A new beginning is possible.

(3) We can *shut up*. Sometimes the most helpful words are the words we do not speak. People in trouble do not always need advice, and if they do, they don't necessarily need *our* advice. People in trouble do not need to be the subject of widespread conversation. When tempted to gossip, chomp your tongue. Sometimes the best we can offer a friend is our silence, until, in secret, we talk to God.

God's Word says . . .

"If someone is caught in a sin, you who are spiritual should restore him gently. But watch yourselves, or you also may be tempted" (Galatians 6:1).

Make it a prayer . . .

Lord, make me an instrument of your peace.

Friday Checkpoint: *Judgment*

Who am I? And why are you laughing?

☞ Think about it . . .

It is a colorful image Jesus paints with words that ought to bring a smile. This guy is standing next to a casual acquaintance. He looks over and notices the guy's left eye is a bit bloodshot. It's watering. The guy is blinking and squinting and flinching.

"Hmm," the first guys says, "a cinder in your eye? A speck of sawdust maybe? Perhaps I can help." He turns toward him, bends in an exaggerated gesture of helpfulness.

The guy with the minor eye problem looks up, gasps, recoils, tries to speak. "W-w-w-wait!" Too late. *BAM!* The first guy has a *log* in his own eye. A plank. A beam. A rafter from some construction project. (Remember, Jesus was a carpenter. He had to be proud of this little illustration.) And this guy with a telephone pole in his own eye is poised to help the other guy remove a speck, a cinder, a dust particle? Instead, he beans him with the pole protruding from his own eye.

Who am I? I'm not the Lawgiver. I'm not the Judge. I am a fellow-struggler, forgiven by God. Now, if I can just get this tree out of my eye socket, perhaps I can assist you with that splinter.

☞ God's Word says . . .

"First take the plank out of your own eye, and then you will see clearly to remove the speck from your brother's eye" (Matthew 7:5).

☞ Make it a prayer . . .

Lord, thanks for the laugh—and the solemn reminder.

Week 11

God's Will

James 4:13–17

Weekend Reading

The Guidance I'm Afraid to Find

What does God want me to do? And what if I don't like it?

I woke up at age eighteen. That is very much how it felt. As I "awakened" to faith, I at first found myself in a religious twilight zone, a halfway point between spiritual disinterest and deep belief. I was beginning to care about God and his ideas, yet, at the same time, I was holding back. I wondered about God's will for my life—a new concern to me—yet this mysterious will was also the guidance I was afraid to find.

What might God expect of me?

What sacrifices might he require?

For instance, I envisioned an enjoyable and secure career. Would he expect me to give up fun and financial stability to tramp through sweltering Africa, Bible in hand? When the time came, I intended to marry beauty, intelligence, and wit. Would God leave me to shift for myself, single? Or worse, unhappily married?

I did not voice the question in these terms, but I wondered—I *worried*: could God be trusted? I had given myself to him. In return, would he give me all that mattered, all that I wanted and expected from life? Or would he just keep *taking* from me, demanding more and more?

I felt that I could give myself to God only if he would guarantee the payoff. Yet how could I make demands of God?

Faith was awakening. But so was reluctance and doubt.

In that spiritual twilight, I dreamed of God's plans while clinging to my own.

"So, what are you going to do with your life?" a family friend asked me. Graduation was now about six months away and I found myself fielding the question from someone almost weekly.

"I'm going to be a free-lance musician," I told her. "I play the drums."

"Uh, that's interesting," she managed to reply, then inquired, "is there job security in that? Do you have something to fall back on?"

"It's what I want to do," I said, bringing an abrupt end to the conversation. I was confident in my ability; I expected God to make me financially successful; I had no interest in doing something that did not have my complete heart.

A month later, when asked the same question by another friend, I gave a different answer: "I plan to go into the ministry."

I think my friend gasped. Perhaps it was a hiccup, or a stifled belch.

"Oh," she said, so obviously surprised. "I had no idea you had become so, well, so religious."

"Things change," I explained. "So do people."

"Will you be able to make a living at that?" she asked, apparently before thinking.

I remember responding as I had to that other friend a month earlier: "It's what I want to do."

I meant to say, "That's not my problem," for I was beginning to think if I did what God wanted, he would manage the details. Major changes were rearranging my life, altering what mattered to me.

(As time and life unfolded, I moved from youth ministry to Christian writing. Music became merely an avocation. Looking back, the progression seems logical and natural. I do not question: "Am I in God's will?" though I never would have anticipated life as I now live it.)

> *"Now listen, you who say, 'Today or tomorrow we will go to this or that city, spend a year there, carry on business and make money.' Why, you do not even know what will happen tomorrow. What is your life? You are a mist that appears for a little while and then vanishes" (James 4:13–14).*

These two things are together, inseparable: our plans and our limitations.

It is our nature to make ambitious plans. We feel strong. Life seems permanent. So much appears to be under our control—our abilities, our education, our interests, our resources.

So we plan to make money, unleashing our entrepreneurial instinct. Or we plan to loaf, idling our ingenuity. Or we plan to do great things for humanity or God, embracing the world and our strength to help.

Plan, plan, plan.

In truth, we are frail and life is short. Through this mist, every breath is a gift.

Alone, we are powerless to enact the plans we devise.

With God, we can frame plans that are wise and good; then watch as they become reality.

> *"You ought to say, 'If it is the Lord's will, we will live and do this or that.' As it is, you boast and brag. All such boasting is evil!" (James 4:15–16).*

The phrase—"if it is the Lord's will" —is not a good-luck charm.

And it is to be more than a PS at the end of our grand plans.

These words say something about us—what we feel, how we believe.

I could say, for instance: "I have this fail-safe scheme. I'm going to make a lot of money."

Instead, I could express myself like this: "I've heard about a great opportunity. If it's God's will, I'll get the job."

The two convey very different ideas. One reminds me that I am great and capable. The other underscores my dependence on God.

Isn't it wise and good to make God central in every decision? Isn't it evil and foolish to keep God at arm's length while I plan my life?

> *"Anyone, then, who knows the good he ought to do and doesn't do it, sins" (James 4:17).*

It's good to give God the credit he deserves when my plans work out. It's good to trust him when life is difficult. It's good to keep him central in all I do or think or plan. It's good to care about his will.

To do less than all of this is to sin.

So I must decide. I must choose to follow the wisdom of his will.

But what is God's will for my life?

That's the question I stumbled over and wondered about back in that twilight of my faith, at age eighteen.

Where will I go to school?

What job will I take?

Will I marry? And whom?

The questions I raised about God's will sound so much like the questions I might ask a fortune teller. Did I really care about God's will? Or was I just curious about the future, apprehensive about the unknown?

Was it God's will that mattered to me? Or was I merely trying to avert future shock?

Whenever I asked, "What is God's will for my life?" the big, long-range issues were on my mind: schooling, career, marriage. This is good. We ought to consider what God thinks as we plan. At the same time, however, I did not relate God's will to how I spent Friday evening or how I treated my mom or what kind of movies I watched.

Do we truthfully care about God's will for tomorrow if we do not live it today?

After all, it is in the day-to-day issues that God's will is clarified. We learn to care about what matters to God in our career, for example, by learning to care about what matters to him in our families. Doing his will in the "little things" conditions us to live his will in the "big things." But if we will not follow God's will today—in friendships, in moral purity, in family relationships—will we ever truly care about God's will in the major, future issues—education, career, marriage?

The future is coupled to the present. How we follow God's will now shapes how we will follow it then.

The difference between the future and the present is this: we *live* the present; we can only *dream* the future. For God's will to shape our dreams, it must mold life as we live it today.

The person I claim to follow said: "Seek first his kingdom and his righteousness, and all these things will be given to you as well. Do not worry about tomorrow," he continued, "for tomorrow will worry about itself" (Matthew 6:33–34).

"Anyone, then, who knows the good he ought to do and doesn't do it, sins" (James 4:17). I know the good I ought to do. I have awakened to his will. With his help, I must live it.

Today.

Monday Checkpoint: *God's Will*

I said, "Do you like the steak?" He said, "Goo-goo."

☞ Think about it . . .

What I love about God is his patience—the gentle way he leads us. He could make abrupt demands; that is his prerogative as God. He could order us around and make us leap to do his every request. He could impose his will on us, strip us of the dignity and responsibility of choice.

Instead, he slowly, kindly persuades us. He wins our affection, our trust, our acquiescence—and he does this gradually. Slowly, our desires change to match his; we discover that they will lead to our happiness and good.

Because this process is gradual, we will wonder at times if God's will for us bears any resemblance to *our* will for life. Or will his plans be frightening, unappealing, downright spooky?

This is a little bit like asking a toddler if he thinks he's going to like steak and seafood when it's served to him at his prom dinner, in fifteen years. It's like asking a five-year-old boy if he thinks he's going to like girls someday. Time changes many things—our perspective, our understanding, even our desires.

☞ God's Word says . . .

"Trust in the Lord with all your heart and lean not on your own understanding; in all your ways acknowledge him, and he will make your paths straight" (Proverbs 3:5–6).

☞ Make it a prayer . . .

Father, help me relax in our friendship.

Tuesday Checkpoint: *God's Will*

In all our plans, where does God fit?

Think about it . . .

Our brains did not evolve from cauliflower or eggplant. They were a gift from God. Even many of our yearnings have been placed within us by the fingertips of God. It is appropriate that we would dream dreams, devise plans, draft blueprints for life.

We assess our abilities, consider our interests, weigh our educational options, take our resources into account. We plan our work; we work our plan. All this is more than understandable—it is responsible and good.

We also have limitations, perhaps the greatest of which is not fully comprehending just how limited we truly are. Our wisdom, our resources, our cleverness, take us only so far. We are, in fact, more fragile than we can begin to imagine. Our very breath is a gift. Without it a mere few minutes, and all our plans are suddenly irrelevant.

We don't need God simply to review the plans we have already made, then veto them if he must. We need his partnership in every step we take.

God's Word says . . .

"Now listen, you who say, 'Today or tomorrow we will go to this or that city, spend a year there, carry on business and make money.' Why, you do not even know what will happen tomorrow. What is your life? You are a mist that appears for a little while and then vanishes" (James 4:13–14).

Make it a prayer . . .

Thank you, Lord, for your hand on my shoulder; your advice, whispered in my ear.

Wednesday Checkpoint: *God's Will*

When you hear the words "God's will," what questions come to mind?

☞ Think about it . . .

To put it another way, if you could ask God three questions about his will for your life, what would they be? Would you want to know where you will go to school? What kind of job you will land? How much money you can expect to make? Would you ask him if you will marry? And whom?

We wonder about God's will. But the questions we raise about it sound so much like the kinds of things we might ask a fortune teller. Do we want to know God's will? Or are we just curious about the future?

God cares about our tomorrows, but his mind is also very much on how we live today. He cares about what we *do*, but his greatest passion rests with what we will *become*.

When I express my desires or explain my plans and then add, "if it's the Lord's will," I am saying, "Without God, I can do nothing." I am reminding myself and others, "Every breath is a gift." I am affirming, "Nothing is more important to me than the desires of God."

☞ God's Word says . . .

"You ought to say, 'If it is the Lord's will, we will live and do this or that'" (James 4:15).

☞ Make it a prayer . . .

Make your will, my will; your desires, my own.

Thursday Checkpoint: *God's Will*

I ask, "What is God's will for my career?"
But do I also ask, "What is God's will for my Friday night plans?"

☞ Think about it . . .

If God's will matters at all, it matters completely—about everything. The near future as well as the distant future. Today as well as tomorrow. Who I *am*, not just what I *do*.

Here's a test.

What is God's will for my temper?

What is God's will for my sexuality?

What is God's will for my relationship with my parents?

What is God's will for my attitude toward church?

These are important questions, because they give us some gauge of our true feelings about the will of God. It is one thing to wonder about God's will for my career. It is quite another to remind myself, in the heat of passion, that it is God's will for me to be pure. I may wonder if I will marry—who will be my partner. Today, however, I know it is God's will for me to respect my parents, to be honest at school and at work. I know it is God's will that I control my temper.

Following God's will begins here. With what we already know.

☞ God's Word says . . .

"Anyone, then, who knows the good he ought to do and doesn't do it, sins" (James 4:17).

☞ Make it a prayer . . .

You have shown your will. Give me a heart to follow it.

Friday Checkpoint: *God's Will*

If I knew the one thing God most desired of me, would I do it?

Think about it . . .

I must pause before I answer. It may be difficult. It may even be painful. It may be the thing I least desire right now. If my heart is not right, I may not automatically desire the best things. Is it any wonder God reveals his will gradually? He allows our heart time to catch up with his. He is patient as our perspective grows and our understanding deepens.

In truth, there is nothing so terrifying about God's will. God's will is that we love him. Because of who he is, that is as natural as breathing. He has loved us unselfishly and sacrificed himself for us even to the point of unimaginable pain. That kind of love prompts us to love him in return.

Something miraculous happens when we fall in love with God. It becomes our aspiration to be like him. This one passion drives us, because we know it is right and good. Our confidence in him deepens. We know we can safely trust ourselves and our plans to his care, and that in doing so, we will be free from disappointment.

What is God's will? The one great thing he wants? It's *you*.

God's Word says . . .

"Seek first his kingdom and his righteousness, and all these things will be given to you as well. Do not worry about tomorrow, for tomorrow will worry about itself" (Matthew 6:33–34).

Make it a prayer . . .

I'm yours, Lord.

Week 12

Money

James 5:1–6

Money Can't Buy Me Love

> What lasts? The kinds of things you would like to have around you forever: love, friendship, generosity, kindness.

Traveling south out of El Centro and through Mexicali, it doesn't take long for broad asphalt highway and landscaped roadside to give way to the dust and dirt of Mexico's poverty. Traverse a few miles; California's mall-on-every-corner affluence quickly turns to the absence of comfort and, sometimes, the absence of even necessity.

I watch, for instance, as a young boy in tattered hand-me-down clothes walks across his "backyard," dry dust swirling at his feet. He passes a scrawny dog and a few listless chickens before reaching the small shack that is the family's outhouse.

Here is a get-rich-quick scheme that works: cross the border and open your eyes. Suddenly, gaining a bit of perspective, you feel wealthy and privileged.

Sometimes it requires exaggerated circumstances to learn what ought to be simple, obvious lessons. Lessons like gratitude, contentment, and selflessness.

I am in Mexico with five friends for one week, distributing toys and clothing, and teaching Bible stories to children, teenagers, and adults, who I soon discover are happy, though they have next to nothing.

No, I must relate this experience more accurately: I am here for only one week, but each evening I board a van with my five friends and head north. Even during this short brush with poverty, we cross the border nightly to sleep comfortably in El Centro, California. Each morning, we return to Mexico. Following this plan, most of our meals are eaten on the U.S. side of the border. A few hours each day are spent in clean, air-conditioned buildings.

This south-north, north-south travel brings me out of wealth into poverty, out of poverty into wealth, for seven days, almost constantly. All of which makes the point more forcefully: confined by their lack of resources, these people have little. While I, through nothing I have done, have much.

Perhaps too much.

Wednesday evening, after our California-side-of-the-border dinner, we return to Mexicali to an outdoor prayer meeting at a small church. The atmosphere is festive and our presence with these people is appreciated. They sing traditional hymns with an exuberance I have never experienced. Every face I see in the dim light is animated with the joy of faith.

I listen. Though my language skills are limited, I hear one message unmistakably. It is the message of contentment.

And Jesus said:

"Blessed are you who are poor, for yours is the kingdom of God. Blessed are you who hunger now, for you will be satisfied. Blessed are you who weep now, for you will laugh" (Luke 6:20–21).

Perhaps these words were on his mind when, several years later, the brother of Jesus wrote a letter. He turned the image around, looking not at the poor, but at the rich. This is what he wrote:

"Listen, you rich people, weep and wail because of the misery that is coming upon you. Your wealth has rotted, and moths have eaten your clothes. Your gold and silver are corroded. Their corrosion will testify against you and eat your flesh like fire. You have hoarded wealth in the last days" (James 5:1–3).

Apparently, wealth and comfort can be perilous.

They can distract our attention from more important things. Throughout the Bible, wealth is often equated with wickedness and poverty with goodness. Wealth has such great power not only to provide comfort but also to corrupt us with greed. Our drive for more may lead us to mistreat the less fortunate. Poverty, on the other hand, may allow us to look beyond *things* and beyond *today* to find our wealth in faith and in the promise of a hopeful future.

Having much, we want more.

Having nothing, we begin to learn contentment.

God notices this: how the wealthy view their wealth, how the poor perceive their circumstances.

In that same letter, James says that God can *hear* money talking.

Money that I hoard for my own comfort, without sensitivity to those who have less, "talks" to God. That money, spent only on me, complains of my selfishness.

And God listens!

There's more: Money *that I should have spent on someone else* also talks. It protests my greed.

> *"Look! The wages you failed to pay the workmen who mowed your fields are crying out against you. The cries of the harvesters have reached the ears of the Lord Almighty. You have lived on earth in luxury and self-indulgence" (James 5:4–5).*

And God sees!

Is this just some guilt jag I'm on?

Am I over-reacting if I take personally a message aimed at the rich? After all, I mow my own lawn; I don't hire workmen, then withhold their pay.

The James letter complains that the rich "condemned and murdered innocent men, who were not opposing" them. I have done none of this. Why should I feel guilt?

Okay, perhaps my guilt is an over-reaction. But feeling self-conscious for having much is more appropriate than feeling indifference toward those who have little. Perhaps it is a first step toward unselfishness.

Think about what matters most. Money? Cool clothes? Flashy cars? The money disappears. The clothes go out of style. The cars fall apart.

Well, it's not quite true that money disappears. I mean, it does. But how we use it is never forgotten.

So what lasts? That's simple. The kinds of things you would like to have around you forever: love, friendship, generosity, and kindness. The good that we do, motivated by selfless concern, will never be forgotten either.

It is amazing that one week in and out of Mexico could leave such an unforgettable impression. I have gained much from those I had assumed to have so little to give. My perspective is far more keen. I understand so much better what it is that constitutes wealth, and it has little to do with *things*.

Saturday afternoon, that last day, is spent on a farm with my new Mexican friends. We speak—they in broken English, I in broken Spanish—making understood references to a reunion someday in heaven. As the orange sun descends somewhere west, beyond the village of Progreso, and as emotional good-byes are exchanged, one friend, Miguel, steps forward, grinning broadly, and addresses me by my Spanish name.

"Hasta luego, San Diego!" he says, proud of the rhyme and word-play on my name.

In my mind's eye I can still see him standing there beside our blue van, in his faded jeans and dust-smeared T-shirt, seeming far more wealthy than I.

Monday Checkpoint: *Money*

Here's a get-rich scheme that works!

Think about it . . .

Cross the border and open your eyes. Perhaps you have had an experience similar to mine. I enter a particularly impoverished area in Mexico and suddenly realize how much I have. I had never before thought of myself as rich, but poverty and wealth are relative terms. Compared to most of the world, North Americans are quite rich.

Yet even in this country, with its plenty, comfort is not a universal experience. On a cold December day I board the subway and take a seat. Across the aisle is what at first appears to be nothing more than a pile of rags, a stack of dirty clothing, perhaps. The heap, bundled there and still, smells of urine and sweat. Moments pass before it stirs. The woman beneath the rags awakes. Today, this subway car will be her home.

In a world where such poverty exists, is it any wonder that God would take a particular interest in the poor? That he would feel their heartache and hold out the hope of future comfort?

God's Word says . . .

"Blessed are you who are poor, for yours is the kingdom of God. Blessed are you who hunger now, for you will be satisfied. Blessed are you who weep now, for you will laugh" (Luke 6:20–21).

Make it a prayer . . .

Stir me, Father, that I would feel as you feel.

Tuesday Checkpoint: *Money*

How can it be that people who have less can sometimes feel more content?

☞ Think about it . . .

This is what has surprised me most. I have met people who have so little yet have the look of wealth in their eyes. They are content. (Others, of course, poorer than poor, suffer much and wait for the relief death will bring.)

Toward the end of his life, Paul wrote, "We have brought nothing into the world, and we can take nothing out of it." He may have been thinking about the moment he would step out of this life and into the next. "If we have food and clothing, we will be content."

Most of us have far, far more than food and clothing. We have food to spare—and food we *like*. The amount of food some of us *throw away* would be sufficient to keep someone else alive. And clothing? Not only do we have *clothing*, we have clothing with the right labels on it.

This makes Paul sound so . . . well, so *religious* when he speaks of contentment. His words set a high standard; could we ever measure up? Would we even *want* to? But in another place, Paul wrote that contentment was something he had to *learn* (Philippians 4:11–12). Even for him, it did not come naturally.

☞ God's Word says . . .

"Godliness with contentment is great gain" (1 Timothy 6:6).

☞ Make it a prayer . . .

Teach me to be content. Make me want to learn.

Wednesday Checkpoint: *Money*

Suppose I say, "Wealth is dangerous." Does that make you want to empty your wallet?

Think about it . . .

Money is necessary. It's not optional. Without it, we don't eat, we lack shelter and clothing. Money is also fun. Life is more comfortable and pleasant when the dollars are flowing. But money is dangerous too. It can be a distraction, diverting our attention from more important things.

The more we gain, the more we must remind ourselves: *Compared to forever, this green stuff is not that big a deal.* Why? Because money is the currency of *time*; it makes things more agreeable *here*. It is the ticket that takes us where we want to go *now*, on this planet. But this planet is only our temporary home. God has better plans for us. The *future* is ours.

We can plan for that future, and we can invest in it now. But if we get too comfortable, the here and now will start to feel like all the heaven we could ever want. We may become so preoccupied with all that good stuff that, in time, we totally forget "forever," until it is forever too late.

God's Word says . . .

"The love of money is a root of all kinds of evil. Some people, eager for money, have wandered from the faith and pierced themselves with many griefs" (1 Timothy 6:10).

Make it a prayer . . .

Lord, meet my needs, but don't let me fall in love with money.

Thursday Checkpoint: *Money*

You've heard the saying, "Money talks." But do you realize who it talks to?

Think about it ...

Money talks to God. "Look!" James said, "The wages you failed to pay ... are crying out against you" (James 5:4).

God watches how we use our money; he watches with great attentiveness. Money is a gift from him. A gift to us to make life more manageable, even more pleasant. But God also gives money so that we can improve life for others. Not to horde it in selfishness, but to use it responsibly—and to share. If God expects us to share, imagine how angry he becomes when the rich take advantage of the poor.

"Listen, you rich people, weep and wail because of the misery that is coming upon you. Your wealth has rotted, and moths have eaten your clothes. Your gold and silver are corroded. Their corrosion will testify against you and eat your flesh like fire. You have hoarded wealth in the last day" (James 5:1–3).

Whoa!

So when is the absolute best time to learn the habit of sharing? When? Now. Before you make another cent. You can sponsor an orphan. You can give money for hunger relief. Most churches have a fund for people in need, and you can contribute to it.

God's Word says ...

Words we don't want to hear from Jesus: "You have lived on earth in luxury and self-indulgence" (James 5:5).

Make it a prayer ...

Make me generous, Lord, as you give so freely.

Friday Checkpoint: *Money*

What really lasts? The kinds of things you'd most like to have around you forever: love, friendship, kindness.

Think about it ...

It is astounding to think that the things that seem most permanent will dissolve and crumble and fade. You buy a car. It breaks down and rusts out. You get a portable CD player. Someone rips it off. You purchase a computer. Three years later it's ancient history. Depreciation is even more dramatic than this. The machinery of your body will run down and slow to a stop. It will most certainly turn to dust. The mountains will fall, Earth will disappear, God will roll up the vast galaxies like a bedroll. Time itself will cease.

Isn't it astounding that the truly important things will live and thrive forever. People, for instance. Death will not put a stop to you. Love will continue—friendship and kindness. Your trust in God will last forever. The good that you do will outlast Mt. Everest.

You say a kind word. It will last forever. You say no to a tough temptation. It will not be forgotten. You turn a friend toward Jesus. That one act will shine like the stars forever.

God's Word says ...

"Store up for yourselves treasures in heaven, where moth and rust do not destroy, and where thieves do not break in and steal. For where your treasure is, there your heart will be also" (Matthew 6:20–21).

Make it a prayer ...

Lord, my life is in your hands, and I am rich.

Week 13

Patience

James 5:7–11

Weekend Reading

When a Friend Dies

Can God be trusted when life brings hardship? And who controls the accidents of life?

The funeral was five weeks ago. The girl was fifteen. And those who knew her are left with nagging questions that will not go away.

Where was God that Saturday night when a fifteen-year-old girl started across the tracks? The question matters to me. The girl was a friend of mine. So are her sister and her mother.

As I write this, the season reflects my mood. I imagine it reflects theirs as well. Autumn has fallen throughout the Midwest. Summer's signs of life are giving way to the death of winter. At a cemetery less than five miles away, there is one final, blazing show of color. Bare tree limbs will soon reach toward the sky, empty as unanswered prayer.

It is growing cold.

Soon it will be November, and thoughts will turn naturally toward Thanksgiving. But there are those who will find gratitude difficult. Those whose faith will be tested still.

Can God be trusted when life brings hardship?

Who controls the accidents of life?

Hardship and patience.

Last night I opened a Bible and turned to page 1034. The New Testament book of James, fifth chapter, seventh verse. This is what I read:

> *"Be patient, then, brothers, until the Lord's coming."*

The words were written to people facing great hardship. Some were poor, wondering where their next meal would come from. Some were sick, feeling their strength drain away. Some were in grief, mourning the death of a friend or family member. To be patient means to hold up under mounting pressure. It means to keep loving God and believing him, even when he seems silent and powerless. It means to wait for something better, though the wait may seem endless.

"Be patient *until* the Lord's coming."

There will be an end to the wait for better things. After the Lord's coming, there will be no further need for "patience." All the pain will be gone. The tears will dry one final time. The questions will be answered or will melt away in insignificance. All that is now so wrong will be made right.

"Be patient *until* the Lord's coming."

That's all.

But that, of course, seems like forever.

Meanwhile, where's the comfort?

I can almost see James as he wrote this letter. Perhaps he put his pen aside and scanned what he had written.

As he did so, he might have said to himself, *Sure, Jesus is going to come back. Everything will be corrected. The pain and grief will end. The questions will be resolved. But it is so hard to wait! What about today?*

What he wanted to say was clear in his mind: Even when hardships overwhelm, God is worthy of trust. But how could he put the ideas across understandably to his readers? Did he pause and ask himself: *Can I think of an illustration? An example of someone waiting for something for a long time, who finds the wait worthwhile?*

I visualize him, deep in thought, pacing the room. I see him, looking out his window and across a field as a man works the soil, then drawing on that imagery. He returns to his table and lifts his pen.

> *"See how the farmer waits for the land to yield its valuable crop and how patient he is for the autumn and spring rains. You, too, be patient and stand firm, because the Lord's coming is near" (James 5:7–8).*

We all know that if you prepare the soil, scatter good seed, control the weeds, and water the field, in time a harvest will come. It may be a long process, often difficult, but it will be worth it. The wait will be productive.

The analogy is helpful. But is it enough? We are not waiting for seeds to sprout; we are waiting for answers about the deepest of life's suffering. Where is the hope and comfort if life feels like winter and you are waiting for grief to run its lifelong course?

James gave the image of a patient farmer. Not only an eventual harvest, but the refreshment of the fall and spring rains. That precipitation is the assurance that a harvest will someday happen. It helps the farmer to hold on as he waits for better things to come. This is my experience as well.

I may face "winter emotions," when God seems distant and life overwhelming. But I also experience "spring emotions," filled with hope. God does send comfort now. It comes to me in a friend's caring touch or concerned question. It surprises me as God mysteriously breaks through the coldness, so that I feel his nearness and love.

Another source of comfort.

Again James lays his pen aside and paces the floor. He knows the perplexity and pain his friends have faced. He knows the questions for which there are no satisfactory answers. Perhaps he tells himself that the farmer illustration is not enough to make the point.

I imagine he thought back over his own life, remembering years of hardship and even his own brother's death. What had comforted him and offered hope?

The example of others.

We often find hope simply knowing that we are not alone. Others have felt as we feel.

James remembered the Old Testament story of one man who lost everything that mattered in life, yet found the strength to keep going. That man, Job, went from wealth to poverty overnight. He had to stand at the graveside of his children. His own health failed. So James reminded himself and then his readers: though it was immeasurably difficult, Job waited, still trusting God. So can we. The wait is worth it, the trust is well placed.

> *"As an example of patience in the face of suffering, take the prophets who spoke in the name of the Lord. As you know, we consider blessed those who have persevered. You have heard of Job's perseverance and have seen what the Lord finally brought about. The Lord is full of compassion and mercy" (James 5:10–11).*

As James wrote these words, then, it was with understanding of what it means to suffer. And what it means to wait for satisfactory answers. ("You have seen what the Lord *finally* brought about.") James doesn't suggest that it's easy to wait in trust; only that God cares and that the wait will not leave us empty and disappointed.

Once last week I awoke in the middle of the night. It was hauntingly still. In the distance I could hear a train rumbling through the darkness. And I thought of my friend. Her sister. Her mother. All of us who stood by an open grave only a month earlier.

When you grieve, you so often feel alone, as if no one in the world can possibly understand your feelings or reach to the center of your pain. In a sense, that's true. When you grieve, you grieve alone.

But in another sense, those feelings are shared by everyone. We all know what it is to hurt, to wait for something better. We may find great comfort from others who have shared our experience.

Even so, questions persist. I do not know why my friend died. I do not know how her sister or her mother will ever make sense of it.

I do know that in our darkness there is someone who feels our pain with us. Someone who loves us. Someone who has the power to crush death itself. In my mind's eye I see him rising with purpose and wisdom and power, as if to say, "We've all been patient long enough. The time of change has finally come."

It will be worth the wait.

Monday Checkpoint: *Patience*

Can God be trusted when life brings hardship?

☞ Think about it ...

Life is not always easy. At times, it will bring deep questions. God understands. He is not intimidated by our questions. He is not flustered by our doubts. Even our anger does not exasperate him.

Life is mysterious—to us. It is not mysterious to God. God may be saddened by our experiences, even as we are, but he is not confounded by them. He is not frustrated by the turn of events, even when events turn tragic. When this planet seems to be reeling, spinning out of control, God's pulse does not quicken. Perspiration does not bead his brow. He's not nervously chewing his fingernails.

When we are fearful, he is concerned. When we cry, he is touched by our tears. Our grief moves him; he shares our pain.

Even so, as each page of history turns—civilization's history or your own personal history—it merely brings us one page closer to the climax of hope, the twist ending you are going to love.

☞ God's Word says ...

"Oh, the depth of the riches of the wisdom and knowledge of God! How unsearchable his judgments, and his paths beyond tracing out! Who has known the mind of the Lord? Or who has been his counselor?" (Romans 11:33–34).

☞ Make it a prayer ...

Father, your wisdom astounds me! Your kindness overwhelms me!

Tuesday Checkpoint: *Patience*

"Please stay on the line . . ."

Think about it . . .

You call a place of business and the automated message clicks on. "All of our representatives are currently helping other customers. Please stay on the line and your call will be answered in the order in which it was received." Fair enough. Some businesses have automated things even further. The voice adds, "Currently, the wait is approximately [pause] fifteen minutes." Does knowing the time frame make it easier or more difficult to wait?

Again and again—almost constantly—the Bible talks about *trust*. Trust is tested by darkness, questions, perplexity. Trust is tested by the long wait. The sense that life, or maybe even God, has us on hold. When the outcome is clear and pleasant, trust is unnecessary.

At times, life will be confusing. God will seem silent and powerless. We may think we have been forgotten; still holding for the call that will not go through. This is why the Bible is so preoccupied with trust.

James writes a letter of encouragement. He writes to people who are undergoing hardship. He tells them what they most need to hear. Things will get better, but first we must wait.

God's Word says . . .

"Be patient, then, brothers, until the Lord's coming" (James 5:7).

Make it a prayer . . .

Father, if it was anyone else but you, I would lose hope. I could not wait. My discouragement would overwhelm me. But you . . . you are the object of my trust.

Wednesday Checkpoint: *Patience*

Isn't it just like God to send us hope and encouragement, even if we must wait for final answers?

Think about it ...

"With the Lord a day is like a thousand years, and a thousand years are like a day" (2 Peter 3:8). Not only does God's *clock* work differently than ours, so does his calendar. His perspective is radically different. He is not bound by time. But he knows that time is, for us, a painful limitation.

"He knows how we are formed, he remembers that we are dust" (Psalm 103:14).

So he weighs our times of hardship and sends us comfort. He gives the encouragement of perspective, helping us to understand our difficulties and, miraculously, the benefit they may bring. He reminds us of his love, his compassion, his purpose. He tells us that the bad we encounter is temporary.

Sometimes God's comfort and encouragement come to us through the concern of a friend. Good friends gently remind us of God's care, sometimes without saying a word. They are simply there. They listen. Being there with us is enormous comfort. This too is a gift from God.

God's Word says ...

"See how the farmer waits for the land to yield its valuable crop and how patient he is for the autumn and spring rains. You, too, be patient and stand firm, because the Lord's coming is near" (James 5:7–8).

Make it a prayer ...

Make me the kind of friend who extends your comfort to others.

Thursday Checkpoint: *Patience*

We often find hope simply in knowing we are not alone. Others have felt just as we now feel.

☞ Think about it . . .

When Christians get together and talk, sometimes they make life sound too easy. You get the impression that, for them, life is never difficult. Doubts never enter their mind. They never face fear. Pain, if they experience it at all, just does not fluster them. Sometimes we don't want to admit our weaknesses and struggles. That's too bad because it makes life more trying for others. If *you* are doing so well, I don't want to admit that I'm coming unglued.

Guess what? At times we all come unglued. If you have questions and doubts and fears, don't ever get the mistaken notion that you are alone in those feelings.

I love the Bible's honesty. I know that Moses was fearful. I know that in a moment of weakness, Peter was embarrassed by his faith. I know that Job felt life had not treated him fairly. I know that the disciples bickered with one another. I know that David could not always manage the temptations he faced. I know their weaknesses as well as their strengths.

And I know that in all of these experiences, God remained a friend.

☞ God's Word says . . .

"You have heard of Job's perseverance and have seen what the Lord finally brought about. The Lord is full of compassion and mercy" (James 5:11).

☞ Make it a prayer . . .

Make me a person who is faithful to you, and honest with people.

Friday Checkpoint: *Patience*

Hey, you, would you like to fly?!

☞ Think about it . . .

I used to think waiting was bad. Now I know it is merely difficult.

I remember reading the Bible one afternoon, and suddenly realizing how much it spoke of waiting. Wait. Wait. Wait. This grabbed my attention, and I decided to look a bit more carefully. My biggest surprise was this: the Bible did not present waiting as something bad, but as something good. There are benefits that come from waiting, if we are waiting for the right thing and in the right way.

When we are waiting for God, for instance, "waiting" and "hope" are almost indistinguishable. And hopefulness is a very good thing.

When we wait for God we are "heard," we are "blessed," we "experience his goodness." People who wait for God "will inherit the earth," "will not be disappointed," "will rejoice in salvation," "will not be ashamed."

In fact, there is something almost intoxicating about waiting on God in hopefulness. It brings strength and vitality to our soul. It lifts our spirits. It gives us the fortitude to keep on going, even in the face of the most trying circumstances.

☞ God's Word says . . .

"Those who hope in the Lord will renew their strength. They will soar on wings like eagles; they will run and not grow weary; they will walk and not be faint" (Isaiah 40:31).

☞ Make it a prayer . . .

Thank you, Lord, that you can make even waiting something that is positive and good.

Week 14

Prayer

James 5:13–18

Weekend Reading

Is Anybody Out There Listening?

If God hears me when I pray, why doesn't he answer?

In Detroit, let's say, a family of six prays about the failing health of a grandmother. In Atlanta, a lonely single mom prays for her only daughter, recently diagnosed with leukemia. Six months later, prayer has been answered; the ailing grandmother has dramatically improved, lifting the specter of death. But hundreds of miles away, the leukemia-stricken daughter is dead.

Why was one prayer answered and the other denied?

In California's central valley, a concerned farmer prays for rain to break the summer drought. His crops are at stake; his financial security is in jeopardy. At the same time, in the same place, a vacationing family asks God for dry weather so their recreational plans will not be spoiled.

God can't please both, so how does he decide? Who gets the favor?

Let's say it is the jubilant family on vacation. Is that fair?

Suppose you are part of a large youth group in Dallas. You go to a midweek meeting where your youth leader is talking about prayer. "'Ask and it will be given to you,'" he quotes Jesus. "'Seek and you will find. Knock and the door will be opened.' Prayer," he continues, "is God's great invitation to us. It's kind of like a blank check, waiting to be filled in and cashed. Why do we ignore it?"

As he concludes his talk, he asks if anyone has a prayer request. "The check is waiting to be cashed," he reminds the group.

One guy, a football player, raises his hand. Call him Rob. "We have a big game this Friday night," he says. Of course, everyone in the room already knows it. "It's been a rough season, the championship would mean a lot. I'd like prayer for that." Before the youth leader can say, "Thanks, Rob," a voice from the other side of the room booms out. "Hey, I'm playing in that game too. But I'm on the other team. If we're going to pray about Friday night's game, I'd like equal time." Then with a sly smile he adds, "Say, is one of those checks going to bounce?"

Everyone laughs.

But doesn't God have a dilemma?

Time to pray? Or run from prayer?

"Is any one of you in trouble?" the Bible asks, then says: "He should pray" (James 5:13). But something eats away at our confidence in God. It is unanswered prayer.

Can we say that God answered a family in Detroit by healing the grandmother without saying he brought death to the girl in Atlanta who had leukemia? If the vacationing family in California claims God gave them their dry weather, don't we have to also say God answered the farmer's prayer for rain with further crop-killing drought? If we say that God made your team win, don't we have to say that he made mine lose?

The Bible itself hints at the problem when it draws attention to one dramatic answer from God:

> *"The prayer of a righteous man is powerful and effective,"* we're told, a point punctuated with this example: *"Elijah was a man just like us. He prayed earnestly that it would not rain, and it did not rain on the land for three and a half years. Again he prayed, and the heavens gave rain, and the earth produced its crops" (James 5:16–18).*

For him, prayer received a stunning answer. But the mystery does not evaporate. Isn't it likely that somewhere in all that parched land, another person, just as righteous, was praying that it *would* rain? Perhaps it was a mother, distressed by famine, cradling a dying son in her arms. Looking back, we know something of the purpose of God; there was a great contest between evil and good (1 Kings 17–18). The grieving mother may not have known this, however, nor if she had, would it have been easy to accept the wisdom of God at the cost of her son.

Even answers sometimes underscore unsettling questions.

If any one of us is in trouble, then, should we pray? Or should we run from prayer with all its unpredictability?

Maybe we misunderstood prayer.

Maybe the whole scheme behind prayer is different than we imagine. It is true, for instance, that the Bible says, "You do not have, because you do not ask God." But it also says, "When you ask, you do not receive, because you ask with wrong motives" (James 4:2–3).

A lot of our unanswered prayer can be dumped in that box labeled "WRONG MOTIVES." Certainly not all of it.

I ask God to end a war or to help me feed a hungry child or stop the advance of a deadly disease or to bring a confused friend to his senses. What if the answers don't materialize? Does it mean my motives were wrong?

Or is there an even deeper mystery to prayer?

The ultimate answer.

In the context of hardship and prayer the New Testament book of James promises that Jesus will return to earth to correct every wrong. "Be patient, then," James says, "until the Lord's coming" (James 5:7). "The Lord's coming is near" (5:8). "The Judge is standing at the door!" (5:9).

If prayer worked like we would like it to work, why would we need Jesus to return? If war broke out, we could ask for peace and receive it. If sickness or death threatened us, we could claim healing and unbroken health. If money got scarce, we could pray in a blessing.

Jesus is coming back as James promised. In a sense, he has to, *because* prayer does not work as we would like it to work. It "works." But it works as *God* intends it to work, a system far different from ours.

At times, prayer may prompt God to intervene, even miraculously. We cannot truly survive without prayer, though we may think we can. But prayer will not sufficiently reshape life. Until Jesus returns we will continue to face troubles.

Even so, the troubles are temporary—and so are "unanswered prayers."

I pray for peace, for health, for security, and the ultimate answer is already promised: Jesus is returning to bring peace. In his kingdom there will be no sickness, sorrow, or death. Every need will be met.

The return of Jesus is the guarantee: eventually, every legitimate prayer will be answered. We are urged to live life as if his return might happen at any moment. The most impossible of prayers could, therefore, be answered when we least expect it.

It would not be stupid to think of it like this: *Prayers answered now, before Jesus returns, are prayers answered "early."* It is not surprising, then, that people who face insurmountable hardship often pray for the return of Jesus. Tucked within the last fifteen words of the Bible you will find the ultimate prayer: "Come, Lord Jesus" (Revelation 22:20).

Until then, we live on a planet so unfair and twisted that we will often be driven to God, knowing there is nowhere else to turn.

The real question, then, is not: Does God answer prayer? It is: How do I live life now, on this twisted, inequitable planet? How can I connect with the mysterious purpose of God until the final answers come?

The answer is both simple and frustratingly confusing: pray. Pray about every concern. Share every sorrow. Discuss every disappointment. Thank God for every success. Give him credit for every joy. Be honest about every doubt. Talk to him when life is most confusing or most rewarding.

Pray and keep praying, whether the answers come rapidly or sluggishly. Whether God seems attentive or silent.

Sometimes dramatic "early" answers will startle us. Other times our perseverance will be rewarded; a long wait will be followed by desirable results. At times we will realize that we have neglected important things, praying only selfishly and shallowly. Sometimes we will be disappointed and harassed by doubt. Life may still perplex us with its inequitable twists and unfair surprises. Yet in praying, regardless of the results, we put ourselves in the best possible position to move away from hopelessness and toward the one who understand us and loves us, rejoices with us and hurts with us. The one who is himself the final answer to every prayer.

Monday Checkpoint: *Prayer*

Trouble's coming. Now what?

Think about it . . .

There is something refreshingly straightforward about the letter James wrote. He has given unmistakably clear advice about hardship, temptation, hypocrisy, speech, judgment, God's will, money. Now, as he moves toward his conclusion, can you see him stroking his beard, running his hands through his shaggy hair, and muttering, "Hmm, let's see. Anything else?" And what does he say? Something all-encompassing: "Is any one of you in trouble? He should pray."

There are all kinds of troubles we might face. There is one universally helpful response: Pray. You're facing great hardship and feel discouraged. Pray. You've given in to temptation and you feel guilty. Pray. You're not sure what you should do with your life. Pray. You've fallen sick; you feel weak. Pray.

There are all kinds of troubles we might face. There are none that can separate us from God. He is at our side through our most profound achievements and our greatest disappointments. He is with us in our happiness; beside us in our sorrows. He is our closest companion when we have done what is right; he will not leave us during our worst times of moral failure.

Prayer reminds us that God is our friend, our helper, our counselor through all that life brings. And prayer says we're glad.

God's Word says . . .

"Is any one of you in trouble? He should pray" (James 5:13).

Make it a prayer . . .

Father . . . [fill in the blank]

Tuesday Checkpoint: *Prayer*

What kind of prayer gets answered?

Think about it . . .

Prayers that are powerful and effective are prayers backed up with righteousness. When God has his rightful place in my life, my prayer is stronger. This is true, in part, because I will probably pray for the right things. My desires are more likely to be in step with God's.

Prayers that get God's attention are prayers prayed by ordinary people. There is nothing mystical about people who pray effectively. They are fully human, with weaknesses and strengths not unlike your own. Prayer is not reserved for some exclusive class of people.

Prayers that are answered are earnest, sincere, persistent. You don't have to master some strange dialect. There are no code words. It does not have to sound like Shakespeare. But the words must flow out of your deepest desire. If you want God's attention, mean what you say.

God's Word says . . .

"The prayer of a righteous man is powerful and effective. Elijah was a man just like us. He prayed earnestly that it would not rain, and it did not rain on the land for three and a half years. Again he prayed, and the heavens gave rain, and the earth produced its crops" (James 5:16–18).

Make it a prayer . . .

Thank you, Lord, that you hear my prayers as certainly as you heard Paul's or David's or Elijah's or Mary's.

✓ Wednesday Checkpoint: *Prayer*

I pray and nothing happens. Why?

☞ Think about it . . .

Jesus said, "Ask and it will be given to you; seek and you will find; knock and the door will be opened to you. For everyone who asks receives; he who seeks finds; and to him who knocks, the door will be opened" (Matthew 7:7–8)

Sometimes, however, we ask and hear only silence in reply. Why don't we get what we want out of God?

The book of James so much resembles the words of Jesus, who was the brother of James. I imagine his brother's words were on his mind when James wrote, "You do not have, because you do not ask God." It may even be that people occasionally asked James, "What do you think Jesus meant when he said that? Sometimes I ask and *don't* receive."

James replies, "Sometimes your motives are wrong. Sometimes you use prayer to express selfish desires." There is no guarantee attached to a selfish prayer.

Suppose I ask, seek, knock—but I do not receive. I do not find. The door is still slammed shut. Then, there is the question of *timing*. "Not yet" does not mean "never." Ask, and keep on asking. Seek, and keep on seeking. Knock, and keep on knocking.

☞ God's Word says . . .

"You do not have, because you do not ask God. When you ask, you do not receive, because you ask with wrong motives" (James 4:2–3).

☞ Make it a prayer . . .

Make me patient in prayer.

Thursday Checkpoint: *Prayer*

How long must I be patient with unanswered prayer?

Think about it . . .

Jesus' friends found prayer confusing. So he told them, pray like this—and he gave them what we now call "The Lord's Prayer." It is a model of how we ought to pray. It's fair to assume, if we pray like this, our prayer will be answered.

How do we pray, then? What do we ask God?

"Give us our daily bread." Lord, supply my basic needs for life. Each day.

"Forgive us, just like we forgive others." Lord, when I fall, don't hold it against me.

"Lead us not into temptation, but deliver us from the evil one." Lord, I need your help if I am going to sidestep sin. I need that help *constantly.*

But even before these three requests, Jesus told us something else that should be on our prayer list.

"Your kingdom come, your will be done on earth as it is in heaven." When will that prayer be answered? Well, the answer to that prayer is the answer to all other unanswered prayers. When the kingdom comes, everything will change. Earth will be governed as heaven itself is governed: by the will of God. The return of Jesus is the ultimate answer to every prayer.

God's Word says . . .

"Be patient, then, brothers, until the Lord's coming. . . . The Lord's coming is near. . . . The judge is standing at the door!" (James 5:7, 8, 9).

Make it a prayer . . .

Thank you, Jesus, that you are my answer.

Friday Checkpoint: *Prayer*

Don't give up!

Think about it . . .

"Is any one of you in trouble? He should pray."

Jesus knew his time was running out. Soon, he would be betrayed, arrested, judged, sentenced, executed. He had spent the last few years with these, his closest friends, and he knew them well. He tried to prepare them for his coming death, he had been discussing it for months, but he saw their eyes glaze over in disbelief. He knew they did not comprehend. In the final hours of his life, the bottom would fall out of their world. They would be confused and disoriented. He knew what they needed. So he told them a parable to show them that they should always pray and not give up.

After his resurrection and return to heaven, his friends regrouped and felt the power of God fall on them. They went out and changed the world. But their troubles had not ended. They would face great opposition. Some of them would even be tortured and put to death. This too he had foreseen, and he knew what they needed to hear. "They should always pray and not give up." Which is, of course, what we need to hear as well.

God's Word says . . .

After Jesus told his friends that story, he left them with this question: "When the Son of Man comes, will he find faith on the earth?" (Luke 18:8).

Make it a prayer . . .

When you return, Lord, I will be waiting, full of faith.

Final Words

Still Believing

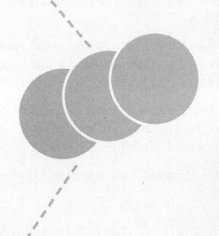

If the Brother of Jesus Were Here Today

So much has changed. So much is the same.

Suppose the brother of Jesus were transported across the centuries and, his head still spinning, wound up in *your* neighborhood. He walks through the hallways of the local high school or perhaps finds himself at the mall.

"Cool robe," one person tells him. Before he can respond, "Well, actually, I'm a bit warm," someone else is commenting on his fashionable sandals.

There's no question James would have a terminal case of future shock. "Chariots without horses?" "Little people trapped inside black boxes?"

"No, James," we tell him, "that's a TV."

"Oh," he nods, "TV."

It would not take him long, however, to realize that for all the changes the centuries have brought, some things remain the same. He would see tears and know we face hardship and feel heartache, just as he and his friends once experienced them. He would notice the way the homeless are overlooked and would become enraged by our prejudice. All of this would feel disconcertingly familiar to him. Perhaps he would shake his head in resignation and disappointment at our lack of progress. Our moral problems would not escape his notice—and neither would our hypocrisy, our greed, our unkind speech.

And yet, if James were somehow transported across the many centuries, there are some things that would not surprise him. For all the years that have come and gone, nothing could hold back the advance of faith. Nothing could silence the church. Two millennia later, his brother Jesus is still changing lives. When life got tough for James, it was true faith that got him through. It would come as no surprise to him that our experience would be the same.

If James were miraculously carried across the bridge of time and dropped off at your doorstep, you would make his day. A smile would spread across his face, a lump would form in his throat, his eyes would glisten, just knowing, after all these many years, you have come to trust his brother.

About the Author

James Long, former editor of *Campus Life* magazine, has won numerous Evangelical Press Association awards for his writing. He has authored nine books, including *Why Is God Silent When We Need Him the Most?* and the first title in the Deeper Devotions Series, *It's Who You Are That Counts.* His experience includes evangelism, youth work, and worship ministries. James lives with his family in the Chicago area.